S0-BAR-179

Elisha Kent Kane
and the
Seafaring Frontier

Jeannette Mirsky

Elisha Kent Kane
and the
Seafaring Frontier

Edited by Oscar Handlin

Little, Brown and Company · *Boston*

LIBRARY OF CONGRESS CATALOG CARD NO. 54-6886

FIRST EDITION

Published simultaneously in Canada
by Little, Brown and Company (Canada) Limited

PRINTED IN THE UNITED STATES OF AMERICA

For my husband
with love

Editor's Preface

IT WAS A CONDITION OF THEIR ROOTLESSNESS that the Americans drifted ever toward the frontiers. The first settlers had been Europeans, and had clung to the seacoast and to their ties with the Old World. But the second generation had no sooner come to dominate American life at the end of the seventeenth century than a restless mobility became characteristic, and that persisted down to our own times.

Most often this drive was westward. As lonely individuals or in families, the hosts of explorers, trappers, and farmers turned their backs upon the ocean and moved steadily onward until the whole continent was peopled. Men uncomfortable in the settled places made their goal in life some ever receding destination that led them endlessly along to the exploration of the vast continental distances. On the Western, landed frontier, the trail blazers, the fur traders, the persistent wanderers, were the vanguard that opened the wilderness.

Some such men also turned their faces northward and eastward toward the seafaring frontier. Among them were the whalemen and the young China traders, men who signed up for voyages that would last two or three years, and in that long interim were content to lead the isolated shipboard life. Among them, too, were explorers who sought out the unknown lands beyond the uncharted seas. These were perhaps the extreme cases of personalities drawn to the American frontier. They raised significant problems as to the nature of the movement as a whole. What tore such people away from their settled places in society and led them to the unknown? What capacities as men enabled them to survive and to maintain themselves away from the grounds of the familiar? The exceptional life of the explorer offers answers enlightening with regard to the whole process of American settlement.

Elisha Kent Kane is an appealing example. His frontier was that of the Northern seas. The elusive goal he pursued was older than America. Yet his outlook and the qualities of heart and mind he showed reveal the distinctive attributes of the American society of his time.

Oscar Handlin

Contents

Elisha Kent Kane
and the
Seafaring Frontier

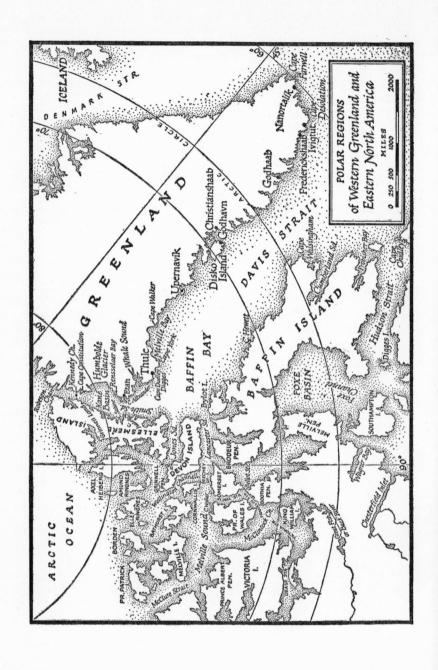

POLAR REGIONS
of Western Greenland and
Eastern North America

MILES
0   250 500   1000   2000

I

Home Is the Sailor

ON FEBRUARY 16, 1857, a bare two weeks after he had celebrated his thirty-seventh birthday, Elisha Kent Kane died in Havana. The news of his death brought deep, genuine grief to thousands of people. But a few years before, he had flashed into their consciousness as the embodiment of the youthful conqueror: brilliant, daring, withal modest and considerate, who wore his courage gracefully, lightly. They knew that during his adult years he had lived in the shadow of death, that he had ignored the shadow and accomplished such deeds as robbed that ultimate terror of its power. The story of his great Arctic adventure — the noble mission to which he dedicated his heart and strength and firm purpose, the fast-moving, hair-raising incidents that had imperiled him, his own escape from the remote polar region, his lively, effortless way of writing that used up his depleted energy — this story had captured for him the whole of America. In him, North and South found a common hero.

So in his death, North and South shared a common grief; a sorrowing public kept a vigil over the body on its long journey from the deathbed in Cuba to its resting place near Philadelphia.

The funeral procession began in Havana, where Spanish genius invested it with solemn formality. The flag-draped coffin — followed by the Spanish governor, his highest officials, notables, dignitaries, and hundreds of foreign residents — was borne to the waterfront. Music, words of praise and farewell, filled the air; then the coffin was ceremoniously placed aboard the state barge and, attended by a flotilla of small boats, transferred to the steamer that carried it to the United States.

As at Havana, so it was at New Orleans. The coffin was escorted through crowded streets, and lovingly placed on the river steamer that took it up the Mississippi and the Ohio. Then, when bands no longer beat out the slow time for marching feet, came the tolling of bells; soft and sad, their sound accompanied the boat, pacing it as it steamed past settlement after settlement; only the voice of the bells spoke for the people who watched from the banks and quietly, motionlessly, were waiting on the landing places long before the steamer came into view, and stayed long after it was lost around the bend ahead.

At Cincinnati guns announced the moment the coffin left the steamer, and houses along the line of march were draped in mourning. A special car, offered by the Little Miami Railroad Company, carried the funeral cortege to Columbus — where, because the train had been forced to inch its way through obstructing crowds, it did not arrive until midnight. No matter that it was night and very cold. The gathered multitude had waited. They, too, heard the steady tolling of the locomotive bell, then the muffled drums, and the dead march played by a brass band; they saw the lengthy parade move slowly through the mist made by their living breath. Moonlight, giving light without warmth, made the scene memorable.

From Columbus to Baltimore and Philadelphia. On March 11 the tenderly cared-for, respectfully saluted coffin reached Philadelphia. Here the wave of grief that had started in Cuba reached its full height and broke majestically. The next day, after a private service, Elisha Kent Kane was buried in the family plot at Fern Rock.

This was the mood that possessed America when he died.

"How and why is this? Of what scene indeed are we the actors or spectators?" a eulogist, speaking in the rhetoric of that day, asked of a silent throng. "This man, whose lifeless form is the object of such emotions and such pageantry, in his life had never distinguished himself — neither on the bloody battlefield as a warrior, nor as a statesman in the halls of legislation, nor before listening and applauding multitudes as an orator, nor yet as a founder or leader of any sect or party in theology, politics, or society. This man was neither of all these, as the world estimates these things: he lived without influence, and died without power. He was but a simple and earnest devotee

(in all his short span of life) to the just cause of science
and humanity; and he died their common martyr."

How and why was this? The question persists. For surely
not every simple and earnest devotee of science and humanity was — or is — so honored, so mourned.

In his day Kane, the Arctic explorer, aroused something
of the awe that Americans later felt for Einstein when he
arrived in this country and Congress delighted to make
him an honorary citizen. Kane, too, heard his countrymen
roar their approval. His quixotic expedition claimed the
same widespread interest that is now concentrated on the
assaults being made on the giant Himalayan peaks, and
his book describing his two and a half years' stay in the
Arctic enthralled a vast reading public as does the story of
the *Kon-Tiki* drift. Such acclaim was in proper proportion to his exploits. His death while still young and at the
peak of his fame charged his heroic efforts with intense
emotion. The long-drawn-out funeral march moved with
the deliberate cadence of a ritual; it dramatized the un-
voiced pity and fear of a people; it was a symbolic cathar-
sis seized on by Americans, for whom always the experience of the pioneer was deeply shadowed by the great
theme of death. This theme Walt Whitman found
words for: "I will show them that nothing can happen
more beautiful than death."

Kane's significance today rests not on his untimely
death which so moved his contemporaries, but on the role
he played in America's seafaring frontier. He explored a

Northern portion, anchoring it firmly in the Arctic, at Etah, high up on Greenland's west coast. His work, now long eclipsed, was brilliant and sporadically continued.

The seafaring frontier is aqueous, oceanic. In the history of the United States it is as dynamic a factor as the land, or Western, frontier. To think exclusively in terms of a Western movement is to deny the presence of those elements which gave the United States its present, far-flung configuration. Clipper ships and prairie schooners used the same heavy-duty canvas. An identical desire to strike it rich sent some to California and others to hunt the furs and whale oil of the seas. The religious fervor that sustained Marcus Whitman's party in their trek to the Oregon country also sustained the devoted band of missionaries who sailed to Hawaii.

Both frontiers were concerned with the same need — the need to earn a living. Agriculture sent its thousands of land-needy people to fill the continental void. Farmers and peasants, they were accustomed to a seasonal rhythm and a sober reliance on fertility; they counted their gain in the steady, small increase of crops, livestock, and children. Maritime enterprises, as traditional to the coastal settlements as farming, required crews to handle the increasing tonnage. Those who manned the whaling fleets and cargo vessels alternated irregularly between shore leave and shipboard; they knew the women of the ports of the world; they accepted the erratic nature of maritime ventures and gambled on handsome returns against odds of risk and loss.

These two frontiers offered a choice to the individual. Those who preferred seclusion and privacy took to the backwoods; those who found it congenial to live with other men in close quarters signed up for the years-long voyages. The outlying settlement attracted homogeneous groups and bred provincialism; the ship encapsulated a broad sampling of the races of mankind, and life afloat enforced an easy cosmopolitanism. A sizable population inhabited the seafaring frontier. Melville listed the composition of the whaling-fleet crews:

"There were Americans from every part of the United States, Portuguese and mulattoes from the Azores and Cape Verde Islands, Spaniards, Swedes, Norwegians, Danes, Dutchmen, Germans, Frenchmen, Englishmen, Scotchmen, Irishmen, Gay Head Indians, Negroes from the United States, Africa, and the West Indies, Maoris from New Zealand, Kanakas from the Sandwich Islands, natives from the South Sea Islands, and half-breeds who represented the crossings of many races."

The two frontiers had different cultural results for the individual. Buckskin clothes are the symbol of those who cleared the wilderness, beyond the most distant store and out of reach of the ubiquitous peddler. In sharp contrast were the seamen, who touched at the emporia of the world. They became familiar with and educated by the elegancies for which Asia and Europe were famous — silks, gay ribbons, exquisite cottons, porcelains, rugs, cunning metalwork and lacquered objects. The homes of ships' captains and China-trade merchants set standards of taste.

And yet, in spirit, the two frontiers were the same. Both magnetized the restlessness and needs and ambitions of hardy, venturesome people — some men turning inland to the beckoning land, some to the oceanways of the world. Both shared the loneliness and narrowness of prolonged isolation; in both there was a merging of races and nationalities; both exhibited a mixture of vulgarity and greed, an essential innocence, good will and violence. Above all both manifested a deft adaptation to the new, an amazing response to the bizarre and formidable.

Like the Western frontier, the seafaring frontier combined many motives. Almost with the birth of the United States, American ships ventured out of the Atlantic and halfway around the world when it was reported that otter skins bought for sixpence from Indians of the Pacific Northwest "sold in China for one hundred dollars." The rush for fantastic profits sent men to the mouth of the Columbia River (1792) and started trade with China; soon no "secret drawer or locker of the world" was free from ships that prowled through the Pacific, the North Atlantic, and the Antarctic Oceans, hunting for whales and raiding seal rookeries; soon the combined demands of audacious American sailors and alert American merchants were marvelously answered when the swift, sure beauty of the clipper ship was created.

The 1820's were the high point in the life of the American merchant marine: 90 per cent of the goods entering or leaving the country was carried in American ships.

The same decade saw Stonington skippers — many were captains at the ripe age of twenty! — steer forty-odd-ton vessels deep into the treacherous Antarctic waters to reap handsome fortunes in fur seals, all the while careful to record their geographical discoveries.

The 1830's ushered in the important, lucrative era of whaling, New England's third largest industry. By mid-century this region accounted for 80 per cent of the world's whaling, and the United States became the principal supplier of sperm oil (the illuminant that gave a clean, bright light), of spermaceti (in the age of candlelight, spermaceti candles were the finest), and of whale-bone, whose unique properties of toughness, lightness, strength and elasticity gave it a wide variety of uses other than for women's corsets.

Kane was born into an expanding, expansive America whose backwoodsman, a figure new to the world stage, had become the national hero. Stories of his exploits as he made his way across the continent salute the back-woodsman as more than a man: he was "not only half horse, half alligator, he was also the sea-horse of the mountains, a flying whale, a bear with a sore head." Or, disengaging himself from the animal kingdom, he "was a steamboat, or an earthquake that shook the enemy to pieces." He boasted he could wade the Mississippi. The Mississippi was rather more than he could wade; but he crossed it, and the plains and the mountains beyond — and so came to where the land ended, California. And that was how and when the Western frontier became the West.

The seafaring frontier created no flamboyant figure to match that of the backwoodsman. Maritime exploration followed Old World patterns, and was stamped with a scientific background. The meanest seagoing ship's captain would not have found a ship, a crew, or a cargo unless he also knew how to read and write, keep his course in a fog, and reckon his position daily. The alliance between science and sailing demanded a leadership based on qualities other than size and power of muscles. Each sea captain was heir to the techniques of navigation, and to the scientific studies which underlay them.

When Walt Whitman celebrated the accomplishments of the pioneers — "I chant America, the mistress, I chant a great supremacy" — he touched briefly, parenthetically, on the intangible, utterly personal driving force which animated the explorer: "(But what is it I started for so long ago? And why is it yet unfound?)" The work of an explorer is greater than his life span — it began long before him, it continues long, long after him. Therein lies his immortality.

Elisha Kent Kane was an explorer, almost the first of a distinguished line of Americans who extended the Far Northern end of the seafaring frontier. Where he went, how, and when — such questions are easily answered. Why he went is another way of asking, what is an explorer?

True explorers are rare. Theirs is the lonely adventure, part physical, part intellectual, part emotional. Like other gifted, ambitious young men, "they yearn for events immense, sudden, and strange." But whereas most young men desire the usual, material rewards, the explorer takes paths leading to immaterial goals, which alone can give him satisfaction. To this select group Kane belongs.

I I

Elisha Kent Kane, M.D.

KANE, WHOSE NATURAL BENT WAS SCIENTIFIC, was fortunate to have Philadelphia as his birthplace. The city still shone with the luster shed by a galaxy of men who had worked, experimented, published their findings, and met to exchange ideas.

These men had created institutions of a practical, permanent nature, enriching their city with tangible assets which increased the scope and aura of their intellectual activity. Philadelphia had the first circulating library and botanical garden (1731). Her American Philosophical Society was long the only scientific society in America. Philadelphia built the first hospital (1752), started the first medical college (1765), and opened the first dispensary (1786) in the United States — evidence that the city's financial position was as pre-eminent as her cultural one.

Kane was aware of his family's importance, and proud. His father's father, for whom he was named, was a successful Albany merchant who married into the powerful Van Rensselaer family and subsequently moved to Philadelphia, then the commercial center of the colonies. In this Dutch connection — in belonging to this family that endowed and gave its name to the earliest engineering and technical school in America, the Rensselaer Polytechnic Institute (1824) — Kane gloried; he was to name the place where he passed two Arctic winters "Rensselaer Bay."

Through his mother, Jane Duval Leiper, Kane was the grandson of Thomas Leiper, a prominent Philadelphian whose fortune rested on the extensive flour mills his family owned, but whose position was of his own making. A Revolutionary patriot, he joined to qualities of courage and enthusiasm a deep, generous sense of social responsibility. His interests and political activity kept him a close friend of Jefferson (for a short while he was Jefferson's landlord), and until his death in 1822 he was head of the Common Council of his city and of his state's Democratic party.

Elisha's father, John Kintzing Kane, was a graduate of Yale and a member of the Philadelphia bar at the time of his marriage in 1819. He became one of the city's leading citizens. His incisive mind and enormous capacity for work enabled him to satisfy his ambitions; his unshakable loyalty to Andrew Jackson and the Democratic party, to realize them. Successfully rallying the pro-Jackson Democrats in the struggle known as the "Buckshot War," he was rewarded with important appointive posts, becoming

Judge of the United States Court for the Eastern District of Pennsylvania in 1845.

Judge Kane had a scholar's mind and sought scholarly satisfactions. For twenty years he served the American Philosophical Society as secretary, a position that made heavy demands on his time but through which he had the pleasure of corresponding with the most eminent minds in Europe as well as in the United States.

This was Elisha's father. His mother, considered one of the most beautiful women of her time, possessed that "energy, nerve, elasticity, and warm-heartedness which became famous in her son." Their home was a center for the gracious, busy, varied, stimulating metropolitan life which Philadelphia provided. To Elisha, the home was all this and more. It was the sum of his father and mother and their parents, their combined virtues and accomplishments, position and friendships. Before the world he would have to justify the blood that ran in his body, the unbroken line of superiority to which he was in direct succession, the unusual opportunities presented a child reared in such a home.

Elisha Kent Kane was born on February 3, 1820, the eldest of seven children. His boyhood had an unruly quality. "Difficult, daring, and desperate enterprises, not only useless, but recklessly wild, under the common standard of judgement, worked in him like one possessed." Through the incidents told of his childhood, there ran the factor of "physical hardihood, and steady, tense endeavor for doing everything that seemed difficult of accomplishment, without other aim, or any aim at all, beyond the mere doing." This "steady, tense endeavor" marked the man as it did the boy.

In school, to which he was sent at eight, his record was bad; he seems to have mobilized his energy to resist the lessons which were systematically imposed and in which the principal demands on him were for conformity. Kane's school behavior was a rejection of a system, of standards, and of subjects imposed from without. For he was studying in his own way. He collected pebbles and rocks, birds and insects, filling a cabinet with them; in a little shack he set up his own laboratory and experimented with chemicals, tinkered with mechanical contraptions, worked assiduously, if capriciously, on his own projects, and read. Some guidance he had, for Morse's *American Geography,* which had found its way into almost every home since it was first issued in 1791, contained sections on astronomy, botany, and zoology, and listed snakes and insects. Geography, as Morse presented it, was a wide, inclusive science; for a young mind like Kane's it had special attraction.

Books on chemistry, *Robinson Crusoe,* and *Pilgrim's Progress* — in that order they were mentioned as favorites — present a consistent mixture of fact, fantasy, and fiction. All printed matter that came into the Kane household nourished his mind and imagination: *Silliman's Journal,* (as the *American Journal of Science* was then called), newspapers, and almanacs. From the *Journal* he had a store of material he could understand and use, and those articles which were beyond his comprehension stimulated his desire to learn. As the newspapers today print ever-recurring stories of sea monsters and flying saucers, so those of the 1830's reported their wonder-hoaxes in the restrained language of science: accounts of exploring the moon by telescope and of balloon trips across the Atlantic, or through space to the moon, were written with a wealth of circumstantial detail that suggested the appearance of truth. The almanacs, "those prophetic handbooks of wind and weather," were studded with brief horror tales of adventures at sea, and their heroes were "a captain from Salem," or "a whaler from Nantucket."

Such activity was understandable; but at best it was haphazard. Mostly he spent his time riding at breakneck speed, or training dogs or climbing trees and rocks and steep roofs. Always his pockets were loaded down with an assortment of stones, dead insects, and unusual lichens; explosions and strange smells came from his laboratory, quick sketches of a curious rock, an unusual fern, lay strewn around his room. If unconsciously young Kane was preparing for his work as an explorer, how was his father — lawyer, scholar of classical literature, and disciplined worker — to understand his eldest child, who at thirteen found school distasteful and was impatient of any control? This passion for sports, this strange medley of activity and erratic behavior, promised nothing for the future. His parents were deeply worried. At his father's insistence, young Kane made spasmodic efforts to prepare himself for college; but not until he was sixteen did he settle down to a routine of study. To qualify for civil engineering, a profession that attracted him, he had to make up his deficiencies in languages, mathematics, and drawing. Judge Kane sought out the university best qualified to promote his son's talent for science.

Jefferson had founded the University of Virginia in 1819; in the last year of his life, he suggested the course for the new professor of natural history. He outlined twenty-four lectures each for botany, zoology, mineralogy, geology, chemistry, and related subjects. The academic requirements of the university were unique: students had to satisfy only certain levels of mathematics and classical literature; for the rest, they were permitted to elect their courses. Here was a happy environment.

The exemption from arbitrary routine and freedom to choose his studies suited young Kane's temperament; the influence of Professor Rogers transformed him into a serious, hard-working student. William Barton Rogers had succeeded to the important professorship of natural philosophy and geology in 1835; he was also appointed official geologist for Virginia and authorized by the state legislature to supervise the first survey of the state. In Rogers, who subsequently moved to Boston and founded the Massachusetts Institute of Technology, young men like Kane found an inspiring teacher. They crowded into his lecture hall and accompanied him into the field where, assisted by his equally brilliant younger brother Henry, the Appalachian Mountain chain was studied and explained.

The year and a half Kane spent at the university was wonderfully fruitful. He was seventeen when he entered, old enough to differentiate between the formalities and essentials of education and to apply himself to both. His childhood interest in chemistry, geography, and mineralogy, his love of strenuous physical exercise, became valuable assets as he drove hard to qualify for civil engineering. The naturalist's world, to which he was formally introduced by Professor Rogers, was dominated by landmarks most familiar to his talents and congenial to his spirit. His studies transformed him into a hard worker and serious scholar; he developed the traits for which his father had hoped.

At that moment, when he was eighteen and a half and had begun to realize his potentialities, when his graduation was but a few months away and his future as a civil engineer stretched out in a long mounting line of strenuous, productive, and noble undertakings — at that moment, the event that changed his hopes, his plans, his future, fell. He was stricken with rheumatic fever; its serious consequences shadowed the rest of his life.

Kane's first attack was painful and devastating. Brought home tenderly, by slow easy stages, it seemed inevitable he would die; the doctors saw that the fever had seriously affected his heart; they waited helplessly, offering little hope, as pain and fever persisted without respite.

He survived. But for what? "The doctors tell me," he used to say, "that if I throw off this paroxysm, I may live a month, or perhaps half a year; but they know, and I know, that I may be struck down in half an hour." He was warned that an incautious movement might prove fatal: "You may fall, Elisha, as suddenly as from a musket shot." To what miserable end had his high ambitions come? Dreadful, bitter months passed. He did not get better, neither did he get worse. Judge Kane knew that such inaction, such passive waiting for death, would kill his son; that he had been given the worst advice for an active, high-spirited, determined young man, not yet twenty. As before the father had found the college best suited to his son, so now he found the right treatment for the paralyzed will: "Elisha, if you must die, die in harness!"

His words and attitude achieved their purpose. They roused young Kane from his bed and took him out of his sickroom. They told him to make a truce with death and find a way to live. With his father and his physician, Dr. John K. Mitchell, he discussed the future and the kind of work he might do. They advised him to give up the idea of becoming a civil engineer. How then might he best fulfill himself? Chemistry, an early love, was closely allied to medicine; the study of medicine, the older men felt, by giving him insight into his own condition, would make it easier for Elisha to live within the limitations imposed by his impaired heart. Knowledge, they knew, could not make him happy, but surely it could make him less unhappy.

From this shattering experience Kane emerged with a new outward bearing. Gone was the volatile youngster; gone, too, the depressed invalid. He was sedate and calm, earnest, industrious, kind and gentle, quiet — but in a hurry. He had to learn everything, see and do everything. Each moment was unique, therefore he had to experience it to its fullest; each moment could be his last, and this knowledge pressed on him mercilessly. Year by year the tempo of his haste increased.

In the spring of 1840, Kane entered the University of Pennsylvania to get a medical training. That fall, while still an undergraduate, his courses included service at the Pennsylvania Hospital. His slight build — he was but five foot six inches, small-boned, slim, and fine-featured — added to his boyish look. The doctor whose junior he was remembered that "at first his extremely youthful appearance rather subjected him to a want of confidence on the part of the patients; but his dignity, great intelligence, and fidelity soon overcame all obstacles of this kind, and he rapidly acquired the respect and confidence of both his associates and patients." Always his appearance was deceptive; an appearance so at odds with his achievements made the latter the more impressive.

A year as a junior physician and he took his place as one of the four residents in general charge of the patients. In March, 1842, he completed his courses and clinical training. He graduated with honors, the foremost student of the class.

Yet several times, during the eighteen months he worked and studied at the hospital, his weakened heart protested at the load put on it; more than once his fellow residents carried him home on their shoulders to be nursed; he returned to his duties as soon as his strength permitted. The severity of his illness yielded to his will. Kane was "unable to sleep in a horizontal position, but was under the necessity of having his head and shoulders elevated, almost to a right angle with the body." He was fully aware of the gravity of his disease, and often re- marked to his roommate "that he never closed his eyes at night in sleep without feeling conscious that he might die before morning." Yet this consciousness did not seem to affect his spirits, or to check his enthusiasm.

April, 1842: Elisha Kent Kane was a doctor; he was twenty-two. With other young Americans he picked bare the summary of the ninety-thousand-mile voyage just completed by the Wilkes Expedition. This voyage studded with tantalizing names fired the will and fed the imagina- tion — Rio de Janeiro, Cape Horn, Tahiti and Samoa, Australia and New Zealand, Fiji, Borneo, Singapore . . . Kane, too, would search until, like Wilkes, he found a new continent, savoring the satisfaction which came to such men: "You feel an exultation, you are a conqueror, you have made a conquest over Nature, you are going to add a new object or a new page to science."

One thing made Kane unique among these men: his health. The physical impairment his heart had suffered did not make the difference; it was his awareness that his damaged heart left him not a day to waste; what he had to do he had to do now, he could not delay, waiting for a better time. "I have always thought," wrote a medical friend who weighed Kane's achievements against the distressing physical symptoms Kane presented — "I have always thought that the uncertain state of his health had a good deal to do with his subsequent course of life, and the almost reckless exposure of himself to danger."

Behind him were the years of his formal education; his future, such as it was, lay before him. He was restless, and his restlessness was not to be satisfied by marriage and family life. That decision he had made while still at medical school, when he confided to his roommate that he would not subject any woman to the fate of being tied to an invalid. Because he could not have a home, he wanted the world; because he could not prove himself husband and father he must prove his manliness in an excess of manly activity; because the ordinary avenues of life were closed to him, he wanted, like Melville, to have "the great floodgates of the wonder-world swung open."

Having denied himself the personal immortality of fatherhood, he was driven to find a way to make his name and bright gifts of mind and spirit live on after him.

I I I

Travels and Fevers

KANE'S FIRST TRAVELS STARTED IN MAY, 1843, under conditions far different from those for which he had hoped. True, he was part of an expedition under orders to go to the China Seas; but the expedition was a diplomatic mission to which Kane was attached as a naval surgeon. His participation and his post were both of his father's making.

Judge Kane, confident that a long sea voyage might repair his son's health, saw in the mission being prepared to open diplomatic and commercial relations with China an ideal opportunity. Even before Elisha completed his medical studies, his father secured from the Secretary of the Navy a warrant to permit the young man to stand examination for the post of naval surgeon. Elisha acquitted himself brilliantly, received an appointment as physician to the Embassy, and sailed aboard the frigate *Brandywine*.

The *Brandywine* touched at Madeira and then sailed for Rio de Janeiro (a zigzag course used by sailing ships to avoid the doldrums) where its arrival coincided with the coronation ceremonies of Pedro II, Emperor of Brazil. The ship remained in port long enough for Kane to travel to the Eastern Andes where he made a cursory geological examination. The next port was Bombay. During the intervening weeks at sea, he was occupied in "the severer studies of geometry, algebra, navigation, and in the languages of modern Europe."

Detained at Bombay some months, Kane explored the nearby island of Elephanta, whose elaborately carved temples were mammoth caves hewn out of the mountainside. In a palanquin he traveled in luxurious ease to Poona and the distant shrine of Ellore, and subsequently went southward over the coastal range with its mighty rain forests to visit other remote legendary cave temples. He crossed to Ceylon and followed the beautiful road that climbs past waterfalls and precipices, through magnificent forests, up to Kandy where, in a sacred temple, on a jeweled golden lotus-leaf the tooth of Buddha was enshrined. He also participated in an exciting elephant hunt before returning to the port of Colombo.

At the end of February, 1844, the embassy ships dropped anchor at Macao, the tiny island in the Bay of Canton, held for centuries by the Portuguese. Here, in its lovely city perched on a rocky promontory, Caleb Cushing, the minister, and his aides took up residence. From there they carried on diplomatic exchanges with the Chinese authorities, elaborate exchanges which must drag on endlessly before actual negotiations could begin.

Cushing's duties demanded that he wait at Macao; he was a patient man and satisfied to enjoy the indolent charms of the town. Not so Kane. He made many trips to nearby Hong Kong and Canton, examined the environs of Macao and the islands in the harbor, and crossed the China Sea to Manila. There his introductions, his enthusiasm, and an energy which not even that enervating climate could dull, led to a Philippine adventure.

Fairly close to Manila, but outside the safe jurisdiction of the Spanish authorities, the long, narrow, deep, deep lake of Taal slices through high mountains. From its water rose an island, a thousand-foot volcano, part of the belt of fire that rims the Pacific, whose crater was like a huge caldron in which poisonous brew of sulphur-covered cones and green water smoked and boiled. No European had yet descended inside the crater to collect a sample of its sulphurous water; no native would even have dreamed of doing what a prudent deity specifically prohibited. Here adventure waited. Kane, with a Baron Loë, a relative of Prince Metternich, was led to the brink of the crater by natives selected by the monks in a nearby monastery. The native escort, only partially reassured by the Catholic fathers, waited while the two men climbed down the perpendicular wall.

A projecting ledge stopped the Baron. He tried to dissuade Kane, who had quickly figured out the one way further descent was possible. Loë and the apprehensive natives held a rope of knotted lianas by which Kane was lowered another two hundred feet. There, untying himself, he went still further down to the edge of the smoking lake. Through swirling vapors those above saw him wait while his specimen bottles filled with the lake water. They watched him straighten up, start back, scrambling uphill over ashes that scalded. Again and again he fell. Finally he managed to reach the rope, tie himself on. They hauled him up; his burned shoes fell off his feet. He was insensible but still clutching the bottles he had filled and some crystals he had collected.

The Baron ministered to him while the natives, terrified, fled. Was his action an act of sacrilegious bravado as it must have seemed to the natives, or was it a brave act designed to achieve some knowledge useful to mankind and helpful to science? Was it a compulsive testing of his courage and stamina, or a sincere proof of his scientific zeal?

Kane returned to Macao. There negotiations had advanced to a series of festivities preliminary to the treaty. Exotic, lengthy diplomatic dinners had moments of high comedy and Kane was amused even when under orders to entertain the Imperial Commissioner's entourage while their chief arranged matters privately with Cushing. The mission ultimately secured important concessions. By then Kane, impatient, had already resigned his post.

His journey home, rich in many kinds of exploration and adventure, was a reaffirmation of his quest for the means to satisfy his need for accomplishment and fame. It was a reconnaissance, a search for a purpose as yet undisclosed or but vaguely felt.

At Calcutta he became the doctor to the traveling party of Prince Tagore, who was preparing to visit the court of Queen Victoria. Moving through India and overland through Persia and Syria, they arrived in Cairo in April. Here the Prince and Kane parted but not before the Prince had presented him to Mohammed Ali. The aged Pasha, ruler of Egypt, gave Kane a special license that permitted its holder to travel without danger or surveillance and sanctioned personal undertakings. It was an invitation to explore Egypt, whose distant past opened the newest, the most exciting and magnificent vistas to exploration.

In 1842 Karl Richard Lepsius had arrived in Egypt at the head of an expedition financed by the King of Prussia. With him were architects, draftsmen, painters, and plaster molders, all technically expert and experienced. His method and his standards established the new science of Egyptology, so brilliantly initiated by Champollion a quarter-century earlier, and prevented it from becoming a pastime for the dilettante.

To a man of such outstanding ability, dedicated to a noble purpose and spectacular research, Kane's response was instant and enthusiastic. He bought whatever books were available in Cairo ("to read with the country itself for my atlas") and loaded them onto his river boat. Accompanied by an interpreter, protected by the Pasha's firman, and with an American flag dignifying his enterprise, Kane went up the Nile toward the Pyramids, Thebes, the Second Cataract — and Lepsius.

Thebes overwhelmed him: "I have been for some days

(three) wandering about in a state of amazement, unable profitably to see anything." Kane was incapable of being a tourist, he was not content to see without understanding.

This is very delightful for a sight-seer, but very mortifying to an ignorant man like myself. Nothing can be more exciting than the intelligent study of Egyptian antiquities. Since Champollion gave tongues to stones, by clothing these wonderful remains with the interest of a recorded history, Egypt has undergone a complete revolution. It is nothing more nor less than a great library of monumental history, where all that is wanted is the patient labor of a reader.

Describing how he reached the spot where Lepsius was working Kane wrote, "I met him seated cross-legged in the great temple of Karnak, sipping coffee and copying hieroglyphics." Lepsius talked at great length with Kane, whose father was known to him through his correspondence with the American Philosophical Society. Kane himself traveled over part of the expedition's itinerary without misadventure. Only as he approached Cairo was he enveloped in misfortune — his baggage, his collections and journals were lost. "Sympathize with this poor, very poor devil, who alone in a sandy desert, rejoices in three shirts, a pair of slippers, and a boat-cloak." At first he blamed himself for the loss. But his self-accusations were short-lived; soon he had proof that he had been robbed: he found his interpreter sporting his watch and chain. This, after a severe tussle, he recovered, but only this.

His unhappy adventures in Egypt continued. A party of Bedouins held him up and, in the struggle, he was wounded in the leg. He felt fortunate to reach Alexandria. While his wound was healing he fell ill of the plague, an attack which proved almost fatal. During his illness he had time to consider whether Egypt was the proper sphere for his talents. To explore as Lepsius was exploring was only possible for someone whose training and knowledge had prepared him to cope with the immense problems posed by the Egyptian records; to Kane it was clear that no matter how great his interest, how indefatigable his labors, he lacked the requisite preliminary studies. He hardly waited for his strength to return before he left for Greece.

Greece, Italy, Switzerland, Germany, France — he went steadily on, he had eyes for everything; he seemed to be seeking; but nothing detained him. In Switzerland he paid close attention to the glaciers, for only a few years before Louis Agassiz had published the conclusion forced on him by such a study; his work had ushered in the theory of an Ice Age of whose dominion glaciers, polished rocks, moraines and erratic blocks were the tokens. Kane would remember these Swiss glaciers when he saw the mightier ones of Greenland.

He returned home. On his first long venture he had been gone two and a half years.

During the winter of 1845-1846, Kane behaved like a man who, having satisfied an itch to see the world, buckles down to his job and cheerfully settles into an ordinary routine. He took a house on Walnut Street and furnished an office; he concentrated on establishing a practice and busily attended meetings and parties. He was like any bright, ambitious, young doctor, except that officially he was still in the navy. Though he had qualified for the post of assistant surgeon more than three years before he had never been commissioned and his name had never been on a payroll. Because no vacancy existed, Kane had been permitted to accept the position in Cushing's embassy.

The winter of 1845-1846 was a time of tension, of a mood to match the newly-coined phrase "manifest destiny." It was a time of waiting while incident piled on incident between the Nueces and the Rio Grande; a time when the United States in a sudden, adolescent spurt added Texas. Gradually and inevitably events moved toward the eve of war. With thousands of other young men of twenty-five, Kane was profoundly stirred. He disregarded his family's pleas to resign from the navy. Though he hated navy life — its gross distinctions of rank, its brutalities (flogging was not abolished until 1850), its meaningless dreary routine — Kane put his name back on the Department's rolls. His civilian activities halted; he was "waiting for orders."

On May 13, 1846, Congress declared "that war with Mexico already existed by the act of that power." Three weeks before, Kane had received his orders, and by the twenty-fifth was aboard the frigate *United States*. He who had dreamed of war service found himself instead on patrol duty to suppress illegal slave trading. He was bound for Africa! His assignment made him "bitterly bitter."

Kane already knew the Africa of Moslem rule and Egyptian monuments. Now he sampled equatorial Africa, whose vigorous vegetation reminded him of the great Amazonian jungles he had seen three years before. At that time Kane had ministered to an important slave trader in Rio de Janeiro and in return received letters commending him to the merchant's representatives. The slave factories that dotted that infamous coast received Kane as a friend. He watched goods being assembled for shipment to Abomey, the great slave center in the interior. Traveling there in a caravan, he met the fabulous king of Dahomey who lived in murderous splendor on the magnificent tribute sent him.

As the frigate coasted southward, Kane was confronted by "the true responsibilities of a navy surgeon." The dreaded East Coast fever had made its appearance. For three months he tended the stricken men, and then fell ill himself. When he emerged from the violent ravages, the fleet surgeon, despairing of Kane's recovery if kept in that baleful climate, sent him back at the first opportunity. In April, 1847, ten months after he had reluctantly sailed for Africa, he was home.

His health was broken and his buoyant spirit weighted with bitterness. He resented the wanton waste of time when he had but a few years to live. "He yearned," noted a friend, "to crowd it with activities which might compensate by their worthiness for its brevity. His opportunity seemed now to have escaped him; and the weary weeks of the ensuing confinement to his sick-room were among the worst for him in his hard lifetime." Not until late in October was he well enough to go about freely.

His first act betrayed his inner drive, his impatience. So intolerable was the thought that the war might end without his having participated, that he left a party and took a night train to Washington. Had a guest told the latest war news: Mexico City had surrendered a month earlier to General Scott?

As was then the custom, with other petitioners, Kane saw the President himself. Polk knew his father and listened as the Judge's son pleaded for a task worthy of his ability, claiming special consideration to compensate him for his African tour of duty. Kane was given an assignment which delighted him: he was to transmit an important message verbally to General Scott in Mexico City. Communications between the capitol and the Gulf were disrupted; a pressing dispatch sent three times by the Secretary of War to the American forces besieged in Puebla had not been acknowledged. Polk instructed Kane what to tell General Scott; to Kane's daring and ingenuity he left the route to be taken through enemy territory. The President wished Kane Godspeed.

Kane carried out his mission in the grand style. On his way to New Orleans he purchased a Kentucky-bred horse, a gray gelding, gallant and high-spirited. Sailing to Vera Cruz with him were "ladies, officers, gentlemen, volunteer soldiers, followers of the camp, horses, and all the lumber of military equipment."

At Vera Cruz, Kane instantly started on the perilous ride to Mexico City. As far as Perote, about a third of the way, he accompanied a party of officers pushing along as fast as possible to catch up with their regiment. Forced to wait at Perote for an escort, he accepted the dubious safety afforded by a large band of Mexicans — robbers, bandits, traitors — in the pay of the United States. "I have determined to trust myself to the tender mercies of the renegade spy-company, Colonel Domingues, and thus reach Mexico (the city) in time for reputation or not at all," was the way Kane faced the situation. Three days later Kane and his murderous crew unexpectedly encountered a body of Mexican guerillas conducting Generals Gaona and Torrejon and other high officers to Orizaba.

The action was short and severe. The two generals, two captains, Major Gaona (the General's son), and thirty-eight Mexican soldiers surrendered. Months later, in terse phrases, Kane reported to General Scott the murderous melee which occurred after the skirmish was over, when friend and foe changed sides and fought savagely: "After the formal surrender of the Mexican party, Domingues, with his Lieutenants Pallasios, Rocher, and others did, in cold blood, attempt to sabre the prisoners. An American officer [Kane himself], upon interposing his person and horse, was similarly menaced and assaulted — receiving thereby an injury of a most serious character and losing a valuable horse." Badly wounded and enraged at the distress of his superb horse, Kane used his pistol so effectively and coolly that he stopped Pallasios and put Domingues to flight. Kane's courage and chivalry prevented a blood-bath; his noble gesture won for his country amity, and for himself friends.

The twenty-five-mile ride into Puebla was slow, painful, exhausting. Unable to sit on a horse, he was placed in a Mexican cart with the other wounded. Still he dared not relax his vigilance; too weak to prevent his prisoners from being robbed and abused, he could muster the necessary strength to forestall a second attempt to murder them.

In the wagon with him was Major Gaona, whom he had wounded, captured, protected and finally, by prompt and skillful medical aid, saved: as soon as Kane had balked Domingues's homicidal impulse, he had noticed that Major Gaona "was bleeding to death from an artery in the groin. With the bent prong of a table-fork he took up the artery and tied it with a ravel of packthread, and the rude surgical operation was perfectly successful." (This incident, as told in a newspaper, drew but one correction from Kane: "His wound was not in the groin; it was in the chest; and the artery was one of the intercostals.")

On reaching Puebla three days later, Kane was desperately sick. Noting his condition as impersonally as though making an entry on a hospital chart, he wrote: "I was attacked very dangerously by congestive typhus fever, in consequence of my wound and the exposure which followed it." Now it was his turn to be the recipient of a lofty courtesy and generous spirit: General Gaona insisted that Kane be taken to the Gaona home, where the General's wife and daughters nursed the young hero with all the care and sweet devotion he would have received from his own mother and sister. A month elapsed before he was strong enough to leave the Gaona home to stand the journey to Mexico City by wagon. The solicitude of his Mexican friends still was with him. "I am twenty miles from Puebla, at the base of Popocatepetl — the rain falling, the wind howling, and some two thousand poor devils shivering under their tent-poles. I am with General Torrejon, snugly housed, warmly welcomed, and awaiting a call to supper."

And so, five months and many experiences after President Polk had sent him to Mexico City, he arrived there. Long before, he had transmitted the message confided to him; he now went to the capital to be examined by the army surgeons. "My surgeons have declared this poor carcass unfit for duty," and yet he would not leave Mexico until the armistice was definite. News and travel were slow. Even as his ardent nature was defining the path of honor, the Treaty of Guadalupe Hidalgo had been ratified, and peace had come. He left Vera Cruz early in April.

Kane's Mexican adventure had artistic unity: it commenced in October, 1847, while he was attending a party after a lengthy convalescence; it closed, a year later, on the same scene. But at the second party, Kane was the guest of honor. More than three score of the city's leading citizens gathered to present him with a sword. Philadelphia was proud that his "casual encounter with the enemy in the Mexican campaign, as romantic as unexpected, was crowned, as an incidental exploit, with the distinction due to gallantry, skill, and success, and was hallowed in the flush of victory by the noblest humanity to the vanquished."

It was now the navy's turn to show how it valued his achievements. He requested, on the advice of his medical friends, to be assigned to the Navy Yard at Philadelphia; he was attached instead to a store ship whose destination was Lisbon, the Mediterranean, and Rio de Janeiro!

Trapped, aboard the store ship *Supply,* "beating tediously between Spezzia and Gibraltar," he wrote a close friend: "I have been sick, and, indeed, am not yet well. The fact is that I did wrong in going to sea. The exposure and wear and tear have proved too much for a constitution already enfeebled by Africa and Mexico and if my cough does not leave me, I shall have to leave home as soon as its blessings are tasted, and spend my winters in the tropics." If his cough was a problem whose implications doomed him to live in an equable climate, he was also confronted with other new and dreadful symptoms. "It was about eight o'clock in the evening: I had for some hours had a stiffness in the muscles of the neck, but locked-jaw never struck me; when, suddenly, a sense of tightness, as if every flesh-fibre of my body was a fiddle-string and some hosts of devils were tuning me up, came over me. This lasted a fraction of a minute and was gone. Of these foretastes of Tophet I had four during the night, and three on shore. I had no more hope of ever seeing home. There was an utter, unqualified conviction of inevitable death. This feeling was neither fear, nor penitential reminiscence, nor unprofitable analysis of the dreamy after-time, but simple concentrated sadness."

Certainly Kane's health was markedly bad, but just as certainly his was a buoyant, sanguine spirit whose instant reaction when not in the throes of actual physical crises was confident, exultant. Three days later, his elegiac sadness was dissipated, and, to counteract his earlier report, he wrote his mother: "That remarkably poor devil, your son, has as an inherent quality of his splendid organization, a principle of resistance which almost makes him think himself 'reserved for better things.' I lost forty ounces of blood [he had bled himself twice!], and took twenty-two grains of opium, and then, bleached to the color of city milk — a pale, whitewash tinge — got up to thank Heaven for the prospect, however distant, of seeing again my very well and dearly beloved mother." Arriving at Rio after a delightful crossing, he "went out into the fields, drank milk, saw kindly faces, and grew better."

Once again it was October, once again he had come back home after a long absence; again he was recuperating. Seven years had passed since he had hopefully, happily started on the first of his far-flung travels. In the mood of a determined young man seeking his true love, Kane had courted fame on three continents and one battlefield. She had flirted with him, but she had escaped him.

Did he then give up the pursuit?

In January, 1850 (a month later he would be thirty years old!) he joined the Coast Survey; he seemed to have accepted the new routine. "Who ever heard of Short's Hotel?" he wrote a few months later, inviting a friend to join him. "A perfect little paradise, looking out upon the Bay of Mobile, and containing a four-post bedstead. Destitute of paint or whitewash or wash-basin . . . Short's Hotel is about the size of our discarded wash-house. This quiet sunshine would not be uncongenial: you could stuff alligators, read books, drink claret, or eat French dinners."

I V

The Franklin Tragedy

DROWSY, relaxed, contented, Kane did not share the mood of Americans then caught up in the mighty drama of their own making. Wilderness after wilderness had been opened, frontier after frontier engulfed by waves of westbound people. The upsurge of nationalism accompanying the Mexican War had been raised to new heights by acquisition of imperial California. No wonder people went out of their senses when news came of the sudden discovery of gold.

From the madness that followed Kane was immune. He had no impulse to join the rush to make a fortune. Quietly he had committed himself to another theater, where a very different play was just then approaching a climax. His interest in the Franklin Expedition, already in the Arctic Regions, was so personal, so immediate, so unconditional, it seemed, as it were, inevitable.

Kane, at thirty, was thoroughly familiar with the attack the British had launched against the Arctic. Since 1818 a series of expeditions had gone out; they were essential to the grand strategy dedicated to the successful completion of the Northwest Passage, a waterway across the top of the Americas. For thirty years the British, soberly, patiently, and at great cost, pursued a dream that had haunted the imagination of Europeans since Magellan reached the East by sailing to the south of the Americas. The dream was entangled with and nourished by another dream, the Northeast Passage that inspired Russia's Great Northern Expedition (1725-1742) to map Siberia's vast Arctic coastline. The dream, by a slight change — by substituting the noble task of exploration for a discredited utilitarian short cut to the Orient — gained new life and persisted.

The Northeast and Northwest Passages! Marvelous creations of too ardent minds; chimeras whose effect was profound and lasting. Before the time of the first Elizabeth, English ships and sailors received a stern schooling in Arctic waters (a man-made Armada could not frighten men who had sailed in tiny boats through schools of mammoth, spouting whales, nor intimidate those who had sustained the mighty thrust of the ice pack). Impecunious merchant adventurers of London gained their first profits from overseas establishments, from fish and blubber and furs (Newfoundland fishing, Spitsbergen whaling, and furs from Muscovy and Hudson Bay).

A worthy group of men ventured into the Northern latitudes. Richard Chancellor (1553), seeking China by sailing eastward, found the Russian port of Archangel; Martin Frobisher (1577) a gallant sailor but unfortunate, was the first to search for the Northwest Passage; John Davis (1584), a navigator of great talent and an astute, audacious explorer, rediscovered Greenland (known and lost to the Vikings) and examined the body of water named for him; he indicated two likely Cathay-leading waterways. Henry Hudson (1610), sent to investigate Davis's "furious overfall," sailed down a long strait into a deep bay; new openings promised further advance, but his crew took mutinous fright, and it was left for others to find that Hudson's bay was a landlocked, ice-blocked inland sea.

William Baffin (1616), a master in the study and practice of nautical astronomy and a courageous pilot, outlined the majestic bay to which he gave his name. Tracing its immense circumference, he noted and named its three waterways: "Sir Thomas Smith's Sound," "Sir Francis Jones, his Sound," and "Sir James Lancaster's Sound"; he appraised their navigational possibilities realistically and doubted if it was worth extending the search for the Northwest Passage. But he insisted Englishmen would do well to frequent those waters — since they abounded in seal, whale, walrus, and narwhal. Baffin was the last of the stalwart Elizabethan mariners.

Two centuries passed before England was ready to follow his geographical and commercial suggestions. When England had finished her civil wars, established colonies and trading factories, successfully fought Spain, Holland, Denmark, France, contained and destroyed Napoleon — when she carved out her empire and made herself mistress of the seas — her energies turned again to the Arctic. There was her ancient, puissant enemy; there her mighty navy found a tradition, a challenge.

During that long period of official inaction, the fur companies operating out of Hudson Bay and the St. Lawrence watershed were forced to extend their operations ever deeper into the continent. To their trappers and agents, the Northern frontier lay where newly contacted tribes were glad to give valuable beaverskins for a trifle — a steel knife or needles, an iron pot, gay beads or bright ribbons. The trapper traveled with Indian bands, becoming expert in the use of the Indian canoe and snowshoe; he traveled lightly, as an Indian, eating fish he caught and game he killed or going hungry; his trips lasted for months and carried him hundreds of miles from his base, yet he felt secure, knowing that wherever there were human beings he too could live.

Such a man was Samuel Hearne (1771). He was sent out by the Hudson's Bay Company from their Fort Churchill factory, to locate and trace the Coppermine River. The account of his incredible, seven-month, overland journey reads as though he were gypsying with a savage band. He accomplished his mission, found that the river emptied into the Arctic Ocean, and, by his wanderings, proved that no strait connecting the Atlantic with the Pacific cut through the eastern part of the Far Northern land mass.

Another such, though very different, was Alexander Mackenzie (1789). Aware of the various facets of geographical exploration — the scientific, economic, and imperial — he explored so that he and his partners could command the world's fur trade. By a bridge of lakes and rivers and portages, he hoped to join the St. Lawrence–Great Lakes system to a river which Captain James Cook had discovered in Alaska (a modified version of a Northwest Passage). Mackenzie paddled the length of the mighty river that bears his name. Unhappily for his purpose, it carried him to the Arctic. Far to the west he caught sight of a lofty mountain range and knew that he must follow another river to reach the Pacific by transcontinental waterways.

Step by step, Kane could fill in the memorable discoveries of the American Arctic almost as they were being made. His father's library would have had Sir John Barrow's widely discussed *Chronological History of Arctic Voyages,* published in 1818, whose map showed what was known; it included the explorations of Davis, Hudson, and Baffin, the Alaska coast along which Captain James Cook had cruised (1778), and a straight dotted line, to indicate the unknown, running from the Atlantic to the Pacific. Only two points broke the uncluttered innocence of this line: points set by Hearne and Mackenzie where they had reached the Arctic Coast.

The geographical problem which engaged the British was of unimagined magnitude. Its solution was phrased in terms of a military maneuver: surround the enemy and close in on it. Over the next thirty years a series of expeditions carried out this strategy.

Some expeditions approached the coast, as Hearne and Mackenzie had, from bases in Canada. The sum of their heroic efforts was a map that showed hundreds of coastal miles, tortuous miles circling deep bays and jutting capes; separated from the continent by narrow straits lay a profusion of islands, whose complex conformation was often obscured by ice that welded distinct parts into a unit.

Some expeditions went by sea. A few ships tried to sail eastward from Alaska (they went halfway around the globe before they were ready to start their actual work); most expeditions tried the passageways noted by Davis and Baffin. Step by step Kane, and others like him, watched the unknown recede as a maze of lines marked where men had explored.

As newspapers carried the announcement of new expeditions, stating their plans and giving lengthy detailed summaries of their results, the Arctic began to take hold of men's minds. The Far North was a region of magnificent accomplishment and heroic endeavor: its strange and terrible beauty was described, its pitiless violence made clear. Exploration of the Arctic Regions was a noble task attracting dedicated workers who struggled to make known the uttermost part of the earth they inhabited.

But it must not be thought that the Arctic was a laboratory reserved for geographical research. It was also a region where men boldly engaged in the day-to-day struggle to provide the necessities of life. In Arctic waters, a fat-short Europe found its first large oil reservoir, and since the seventeenth century Arctic whaling had been profitable; the nineteenth century witnessed the phenomenal rise of American whaling. By 1850 this had assumed a position of economic and industrial importance — almost twenty thousand officers and men manned a whaling fleet of more than seven hundred ships. By that time American whalers were supplying sperm oil and spermaceti candles, whalebone and ambergris, to the domestic market and to most of the European ones.

The whaling trade flourished in small provincial ports between Provincetown on Cape Cod and Sag Harbor on Long Island. Its greatest concentration was at Nantucket and New Bedford. Whaling, New England's third most important industry, was outranked by the long-established shoe manufacture and by the cotton factories. The needs of the whaling industry created other trades: shops where harpoons, lances, and cutting spades were forged, and shops that processed whaling products, shipyards to build and repair the broad-beamed, bluff-bowed, square-rigged "blubber hunters" and whaleboats, beautifully fast and seaworthy; ship chandlery, businesses supplying cordage, canvas and other items of ship furniture; capacious sail lofts where the canvas was properly cut and sewed; ropewalks that prepared whale line, the aristocrat of all ropes; and a multitude of sheds for blacksmiths, blockmakers, coopers, and the host of other skills serving the industry.

Yankee whalers followed where successive British expeditions penetrated Arctic waters north of America from the Bering Sea as well as from Baffin Bay. They sought the whalebone whale — or, as it is also called, the "right whale" — and filled their ships with rich cargoes when they hunted in waters where before no ships had hunted. The need and rewards for finding unexploited waters often made a whaler turn explorer. Whaling and Northern exploration had a centuries-long association; mutually satisfactory, they supported one another in giving to men intellectual incentives and economic motivation.

In 1842 another kind of investigator made his presence felt in Far Northern regions: the scientist-philosopher who, remaining quietly in his study, gave coherence and meaning to the separate yet related efforts of the field explorer and seagoing worker.

In that year, Lieutenant Matthew Fontaine Maury, U.S.N., was placed in charge of the Depot of Charts and Instruments at the National Observatory. He had a scientific interest in navigation and a bold creative imagination — by training and inclination he was admirably qualified to understand the needs of that seafaring age. The time had come, he was convinced, when it was possible to study those elements of primary importance to sail-powered ships: the winds and currents of the oceans. Maury proposed to map the elusive and the ephemeral "by putting down on a chart the tracks of many vessels on the same voyage, but at different times, in different years, and during all seasons, and by projecting along each track the winds and currents daily encountered."

Navigators thereafter, "by consulting this chart, would have for their guide the results of the combined experiences of all whose tracks were thus pointed out."

To each ship captain, whatever his ship, wherever bound, Maury made a proposition. If the captain would make regular, specific observations while at sea and, at the end of the cruise, send an abstract of his log to the Depot of Charts and Instruments, he would receive in return, free of charge, a copy of the chart and sailing directions. The plan had a wide acceptance; and Maury was thus easily able to recruit "more than a thousand navigators engaged day and night, and in all parts of the oceans, in making and recording observations according to a uniform plan." With the oceans as his laboratory and a far-flung staff of interested assistants, he examined the accumulated data that began to flow into his office.

It was natural for Maury to include captains of whaling ships. Since whalers could only hazard an opinion about the distribution of the whales (the different ones yielded different products), Maury also asked for permission to see their logbooks. These were complete though primitive accounts of a business venture; they noted the location, kind, size, number and yield of each whale killed. Great numbers of logbooks were examined, and their findings tabulated.

"In 1847, material sufficient having been collected," Maury could deduce that since "it is physically as impossible for [the right, or whalebone, whale] to cross the equator, as it would be to cross a sea of fire . . . the

right whales of Behring's Strait and the whales of Baffin's
Bay are probably the same animals; and if so the conclusion is almost inevitable that there is at times, at least,
open water communication through the polar regions between the Atlantic and Pacific Oceans; for this animal
. . . could not pass from one ocean to another unless by
way of the Arctic regions." A few years later, Maury
added another reason for presuming the existence of
an open waterway: "It is known that whales cannot travel
under the ice for such a great distance as is that from
one side of the continent to the other."

By 1847 Maury was convinced that the Northern whalebone whale, confined as he was to the chill waters of the
North Temperate Zone and Arctic Regions, demonstrated that the long-sought Northwest Passage did exist.
It was known and used by the whalebone whale.

This fact and this date have an unconsciously cruel
meaning. The year 1847 was spent by the Franklin Expedition — the last, the most splendid, the most hopeful
and ambitious of the British expeditions directed to the
discovery of Arctic America — in a desperate search for
that waterway which led from Baffin Bay to Bering Strait.

The expedition had sailed from England on May 19,
1845. Two stout vessels, the *Erebus* and *Terror,* were
ordered to accomplish the "Passage to the Pacific."

A vast amount of preparatory work promised success
to the venture; how vast and how detailed could be appreciated by comparing the map in Sir John Barrow's
Northern Regions published in 1846 with that in his

earlier book of 1818. The naïve dotted line had been replaced by a coastline; only a few small unknown areas
stretched between Bering Strait and Baffin Bay. The conformation of islands and waterways cluttering the huge
area north of the continent was in large measure understood; the North Magnetic Pole, that sent the compass
needle spinning wildly, had been located; and English
ships had already crossed the meridian at 110° West of
Greenwich before ice blocked their further advance. To
increase the assurance of success, the men who mapped
the coastline found confirmation, from the tides and currents, that waterways connected the Atlantic with the Pacific.

To deal handsomely with an honored enemy, the Admiralty gave the command to Sir John Franklin. His
excellent overland journeys made twenty years before and
his sentiments — "Nothing is dearer to my heart than the
completion of the survey of the northern coast of America
and the accomplishment of the Northwest Passage" —
earned him the post. The navy's finest officers, young men
with reputations won in the China War, in the Arctic,
in Africa and Australia, were chosen to sail with him; the
sailors were picked for the occasion as for a decoration.

The expedition sailed with the pride a conqueror as-
sumes when he goes forth to accept the surrender of a
valiant foe. How long it would take to reach the Pacific
was the only question.

At home, 1846 passed in a confident mood. Worry and
apprehension only appeared as 1847 came to a close. Could

something have happened? Where, in that enormous area, were they held? Then, as doubts mounted, other questions poured out. Were they trapped? What of the 129 men? Were they well and fit? Had they lost their ships in the ice? By what route could they escape? Where would they be encamped? Since there was no means of communication, fear for the expedition had been slow in finding acceptance; and so it was not until 1848 that the search got started.

The Franklin Search was one of the greatest man-hunts ever staged. People in Europe and America were caught and held in sympathy for one hundred and twenty-nine men lost, suffering, perhaps dying, in the North. It is almost as though their combined compassion powered the searching parties that left for the rescue.

Lady Jane Franklin, wife of the commander, felt the force and spontaneity of the public's pity, but she knew that pity, no matter how strong, is soon spent. Her task, she realized, was to maintain it, to keep the need for rescue on the public conscience. She rallied her husband's former Arctic companions; she wrote innumerable letters to the papers, reminding her countrymen of the urgent need to act and act quickly; respectfully but insistently she petitioned the Lords of the Admiralty to lift the icy siege in which the expedition was held; and she gave freely of her own funds to send out private searching vessels.

By 1848 three rescue parties sailed to free Sir John. The initial effort was well thought out; from east, south, and west, by sea and by land, three different parties took assigned routes which would converge on the lost expedition. Not until the following year was it known that they had failed: unusually heavy ice, unseasonable gales, had stopped them; the Arctic had turned back this brave three-pronged attempt. Tension sharpened fear — people now were apprehensive lest they be too late. It would be 1850 before another major action could be sent out; five years would have passed since Sir John sailed — a long, long time to be lost in the Arctic.

The Arctic's brusque rebuff aroused Great Britain. That spring (1849) Parliament offered a reward of twenty thousand pounds for the discovery and relief of the ships and half that sum for the discovery and relief of any of the crews or for ascertaining their fate. As soon as the reward was voted, Lady Jane sent a cry for help across the Atlantic, addressing an appeal to the newly inaugurated president, General Zachary Taylor, calling on him as the leader of a "kindred people to join heart and mind in the enterprise of snatching the lost navigators from a dreary grave." His sympathetic reply did not satisfy her; she had not aimed at starting a correspondence, she wanted to recruit ships and searchers. The following December she again wrote. This time the President transmitted her letters to Congress and asked for appropriations to fit out "an expedition to proceed in search of the missing ships" with officers and crews.

Hardly a more unfortunate moment could have been chosen to ask congressional leaders to act quickly, decisively, and in unison. The immediate problem before them was how to extend statehood to California. (Should it be free? Should it be slave?) The President's recommendation for funds for an Arctic search was hardly heard by men awaiting the considered words which Henry Clay, John C. Calhoun, and Daniel Webster were to pronounce on the proposed compromise. During the first weeks and months of 1850, everything else was pushed aside — the same weeks and months for preparations to start if a rescue expedition was to be sent.

As one looks back, it seems inconceivable that the fate of a British expedition lost while on a quixotic search for a useless waterway should have received any attention in the United States. For most people the question being argued in Congress was an issue to be hotly and bitterly discussed. It had not become the compromise of 1850, one of the crucial steps that led to war; it was not the only topic that enlisted men's emotions and filled their thoughts. There were Lady Franklin's appeals. To some men her words had a personal, immediate, more urgent sound. Elisha Kent Kane was one; another was the shipping magnate, Henry Grinnell (1799-1874).

Grinnell, the son of a merchant and sailing master, was born in New Bedford. He knew at first hand what Melville described for other Americans: New Bedford, the opulent town whose areas of back country "are enough to frighten one, they look so bony," and without whose large profitable whaling fleet the town itself would "perhaps have been in as howling a condition as the coast of

Labrador." To his fellow countrymen, accustomed to think of land as wealth, Melville proclaimed that the patrician houses and flowery gardens of New Bedford "were harpooned and dragged up hither from the bottom of the sea"; that there "fathers, they say, give whales for dowers to their daughters and portion off their nieces with a few porpoises apiece." From childhood on, Grinnell heard tales of fortunes found in the Far North. The enterprising, canny, New Bedford whalers did not confine their hunt to the mammoth, globe-trotting sperm whales that visit the warmer waters of the earth; they fished in Baffin Bay and Bering Strait when the world market offered the largest returns for products made from the right, or whalebone whale.

On the retirement of his older brother, Moses, in 1850, Henry Grinnell assumed active management of Grinnell, Minturn & Company, one of New York City's strongest shipping firms. To Lady Jane Franklin's plea he responded enthusiastically. His early interest in Northern waters, his close mercantile ties with Great Britain, his lifelong concern with ships and the men who sailed them, prompted him to offer the government two ships to enable the United States to join in the search. Availing itself of Grinnell's liberality and gesture of international good will, Congress quickly (May 2, 1850) passed the bill necessary to man and outfit the ships; the expedition was placed under the care of the Navy Department, whose laws and regulations were to be maintained.

Even as Kane was engaged on the Coastal Survey, writ-

ing contentedly from his languorous retreat overlooking
Mobile Bay, the news of Lady Jane's appeal moved him
to action. He offered his services to any expedition. On
March 24, because the navy had "given my 'volunteer'
the slighting answer of silence, leaving me the simple
satisfaction of having done as I do," he planned a leisurely
homeward trip toward the end of June. Before the mail
brought news of Grinnell's offer and Congress's acceptance, before Kane had time to fret at being deprived
of a part in an errand of mercy, he was jolted from his
unhappy peace.

On the 12th of May while bathing in the tepid waters of
the Gulf of Mexico, I received one of those courteous little
epistles from Washington which the electric telegraph has
made so familiar to naval officers. It detached me from the
coast-survey, and ordered me to "proceed forthwith to New
York for duty upon the Arctic Expedition."

Thus he starts his account of the *United States Grinnell
Expedition in Search of Sir John Franklin*. In the same
breathless tone, he tells:

Seven and a half days later, I had accomplished my overland journey of thirteen hundred miles, and in forty hours
more our squadron was beyond the limits of the United States:
the Department had calculated my travelling-time to a nicety.

During the fraction of a day that was left to me at New
York, I strove assiduously to secure a few implements for
scientific observation, as well as to get together the elements
of an Arctic wardrobe. I had, of course, the zealous aid of
Mr. Grinnell . . . but I could not help being struck with the
universal sympathy displayed toward our expedition. I collected as I could some simple instruments for thermal and
magnetic registration, which would have been of use if they

had found their way on board. A very few books for the dark hours of winter, and a stock of coarse woolen clothing, re-enforced by a magnificent robe of wolf-skins, that had wandered down to me from the snow drifts of Utah, constituted my entire outfit; and with these I made my report to Commodore Salter at the Brooklyn Navy Yard.

V

Summer:

The Search for the Lost Men

KANE WAS DISMAYED when he saw the ships Grinnell had given the expedition. At the Brooklyn Navy Yard, hidden beneath a projecting wharf, were two little hermaphrodite brigs, so-called because they were square-rigged in the foremast and fore-and-aft rigged on the mainmast. Looking down at the *Advance*, of 144 tons, and the *Rescue*, of 91 tons, Kane could not help thinking that they seemed to be "more like a couple of coasting schooners than a national squadron bound for a perilous and distant sea."

The *Advance*, his immediate home, was carefully selected. Speed was secondary to strength — her bow had seven feet of solid timber to give her some authority in her fight with the ice; she was easy to maneuver and had ample storage room to hold their three-year supplies. Built to transport machinery, her hull was uncommonly tough and her interior, padded with tarred felt and lined with cork, exceptionally dry; and, to add to her other qualifications for Arctic work, her rudder was so constructed that it could be taken on board and replaced in a few minutes.

On the equipment supplied by the navy, Kane was most tactful, recording only the "heterogeneous collection of obsolete old carbines, with the impracticable ball-cartridges that accompanied them." The most glaring defects were remedied through the energy and resourcefulness of the commander, Lieutenant Edwin De Haven, and the "exhaustless liberality of Mr. Grinnell." De Haven, four years older than Kane, had served on the Wilkes Expedition and learned ice-navigation in Antarctic waters. This training and his own verve and daring made his handling of the *Advance* a fact to be reckoned with in the tense moments they were to know.

Two additional officers and thirteen men manned the brig; Kane labeled himself "that noneffective limb, the doctor." With the officers and crew of the *Rescue,* the total number in the expedition was thirty-three.

Kane, as a traveler of standing, prepared himself for living in close, crowded quarters and for the conditions he would meet in the Far North. Privacy, an essential, was secured, and a modicum of comfort; his bunk, a space six feet by two feet eight in horizontal dimensions, offered both. "My first care was to keep water out, my second to make it warm." A bundle of tacks, and a few yards of India-rubber cloth, made an impenetrable casing over the entire woodwork, over which were laid the Mormon wolfskin, and "a somewhat ostentatious Astracan fur cloak." Two little wooden shelves housed a scanty

library, and a third supported a reading lamp or a "Ber-
zelius' Argand" to be lighted when the dampness made
some heat necessary. A watch and a thermometer hung
from nails, while his ink-bottle was suspended "pendu-
lum fashion, from a hook." To a long string he fastened
a toothbrush, a comb, and a hairbrush.

"Now when all these distributions had been happily
accomplished, and I crawled in from the wet, and cold,
and disorder of without, through a slit in the India-
rubber cloth, to the very center of my complicated resources, it would be hard for anyone to realize the quantity of comfort which I felt I had manufactured. My lamp
burned brightly; little or no water distilled from the roof;
my furs warmed me into satisfaction."

There was something disarming and endearing about
this Saint George-like errand of mercy. Two tiny brigs, a
gallant, capable captain, a miscellany of men and motives,
sailed into the unknown to effect a rescue, steering for
the stronghold of ice and cold where men, strangers to
all but brothers in their mortality, had been caught. And
Kane? De Haven, looking with careful eye over his equipment, his crew, and supplies, hoped that the thin, frail,
seasick little doctor would not collapse before the ship
made Greenland, from where he could send him back.
Kane himself, elated that he was part of the expedition
delighted with his cocoon of privacy and comfort, but
violently seasick, settled down to write his journal.

Sailing toward the end of May, 1850, Kane was at last
heading for the high destiny he had sought. His journal

has the incorrigible freshness of a man who is seeing a new world. He has a story to tell and wonders to recount; and though he has read what other men have described, and their names are associated with specific places, his own impressions of the Northern regions fill him and overflow in his pages. No matter that he had read widely and wisely — this voyage, the First Grinnell Expedition, introduced Kane to a world to whose strangeness and majestic beauty he responded.

Even before they reached Greenland water, the Arctic hailed them. One night they collided with an iceberg; they thumped hard, but slid smoothly enough into open water afterwards. Two days later, a school of whales — "great, crude, wallowing sea-hogs, snorting out fountains of white spray" — tumbled porpoise-fashion one over another about the vessel. Before them lay Davis Strait.

Kane, looking at the watery world through eyes which had studied Maury, saw in a southward-drifting piece of wood "the beneficial adaptation of ocean currents to the wants of man." For this driftwood was "the offcast of the great Siberian and American rivers" in a current that relentlessly carried ice fields and icebergs and unwilling ships southward toward the Atlantic.

"Our Arctic day has commenced," he wrote on June 17. "Last night we read the thermometer without a lantern, and the binnacle was not lighted up. . . . The words night and day begin to puzzle me, as I recognize the arbitrary character of the hour cycles that have borne these names." As Greenland's coast came into sight, he was once again the geologist, aware "that these apparently destitute islands contributed their part to the varied and peculiar flora of the Arctic regions."

At the Whalefish Islands, at Disko, their first port, they had their first contact with Eskimos. While waiting to be rowed ashore, Kane saw "something like a large Newfoundland dog" that had "a queer movement, as of two flapping wings, which acting alternately on either side, seemed to urge it through the water." It was a kayak with its "black-locked" Eskimo. A kayak in the water, propelled by an Eskimo, is a thing alive; "one impulse seemed to control both. Indeed, even for a careful observer, it was hard to say where the boat ended or the man began."

But the Eskimo settlement! Some forty-odd men, women, and children, the children yelling, flanked by crowds of howling dogs, evoked nothing but disgust. This first meeting and Kane's reaction are worth remembering: "Offal was strewn around without regard to position; scabs of drying seal-meat were spread over the rocks; oil and blubber smeared everything, from the dogs' coats to their masters'; animal refuse tainted all we saw." The habitations were worse. Within a summer tent, a little area of six feet by eight, Kane counted a father, mother, grandfather, and four children, a teakettle, a rude box, two rifles, and a litter of puppies. A time would come when he would envy these people their oil- and blubber-smeared garments, their litters of puppies and howling dogs; when he would gratefully add his own body to a crowded Eskimo dwelling.

At Disko they had news that a British squadron of four ships under the command of Commodore Austin had already preceded them in sailing westward toward Lancaster Sound. On the twenty-ninth of June they left Whale-fish Islands and two days later encountered their first heavy ice. "From this date really commenced the characteristic voyaging of a Polar cruise." Before them lay the Middle Ice, and beyond it the American coast.

The Middle Ice, the essential feature of Baffin Bay, is the awesome remains of the winter pack, the thick, solid ice that covers the waters of that entire region. Reduced by the ardent Arctic summer with its continuous sun, the accelerated drift toward the Atlantic, and warm, subsurface currents, the implacable winter ice becomes a "patchwork composed of all sorts of ice, diversified in pattern, age and condition, and varying in size from small fragments to 'floes' or fields, so limited that the eye defines their extent." The floes form the basis of the pack. Their thickness ranges from a few inches to many feet, and their diameter is often many miles. "At the margins of the floes, where their ragged edges have come into grinding contact, the ice is piled up in ridges that streak the surface like the mounds of a recently-ditched meadow. These are the hummocks." Great bergs of every shape were tangled in this floating field.

Running between the coast and the pack, the *Advance*

came to Omanak Fiord, "the most remarkable locality in the *genesis* of icebergs on the face of the globe." In one evening Kane counted no less than two hundred and forty of primary magnitude. This massive discharge from the Greenland icecap dwarfed the Alpine glaciers; and Kane, mindful of the Agassiz theory, felt he had sailed back into the Ice Age.

To reach the western waters of Baffin Bay, they had to cross this Middle Ice. Kane lists three crossings. The Southern Passage, at about 68°, is a possible route to be used late in the season; the Middle Passage, from 68° to 74° — the most hazardous — is rarely tried and rarely with success; the Northern Passage, or North Water, north of 74°, is the highway preferred by whalers "who possess an admirable tact in ice navigation." To reach this, "a mysterious region of terrors must be transversed — Melville Bay — notorious in the annals of whalers for its many disasters." The dangers of Melville Bay were still hearsay to Kane, as they pursued their way "flapping lazily alongside of the 'pack' and sometimes forcing an opening through its projecting tongues." Intellectually and emotionally he could respond to the ever-changing wonders of ice and water and light; his journal is filled with descriptions of the beauty of the icebergs, "so slumberous and so pure, so massive yet so evanescent, so majestic in their cheerless beauty, without any of the salient points which give character to description, that they seemed to me material for a dream."

During that first week in July the circuit around the

dangerous pack was idyllic, worthier of the Bay of Naples than of Baffin. Their progress was uninterrupted; the pack stood a good thirty miles offshore, the space between was clear, and they went as upon a great river. When "a large, vacant sheet of water showed itself to the westward, penetrating the ice as far as the eye could reach," De Haven yielded to the temptation of trying the Middle Passage.

It began hopefully enough. Occasionally they were forced to cut and bore their way, but until noon they sailed through loose streams until, as they thought, they came to open water; at six knots an hour they felt as though they were racing along. "By four in the afternoon, after placing at least fifty miles between us and the coast, the leads began to close around us." Within an hour they were stopped. The next morning found them fast in summer ice. "Fast! Around us a circle of snow-covered ice, streaked with puddles of dark water, and varied (alas for the variety!) by the very distant looming of some icebergs. In the center of this dreariness are two vessels — *Advance* and *Rescue*." The date was July 8; until the twenty-ninth they stayed in the pack though they resorted to anything that might free them from the ice — boring, hauling, warping.

For the benefit of fireside navigators, Kane described these techniques. De Haven, "loth to relinquish his hopes, determined to *bore*. This operation continued throughout the night — all hands jumping upon the floes, and working away with crow-bar, boat-hook, ice-anchor, and warp-

ing lines. The result of all this labor was that the two
vessels made about three quarters of a mile into deeper
entanglement; and now, at 11 P.M., we are fast in the apparent centre of a solid sea."

The season was still young, the experience still novel,
and Kane could comment breezily on their efforts to extri-
cate themselves and go forward.

A couple of hands, under orders, of course, seize an iron
hook or ice-anchor, of which we have two sizes, one of forty,
and another of about a hundred pounds. With this they jump
from the bows and *plant it* in the ice ahead, close to the edge
of the crack along which we wish to force our way. Once fast,
you slip a hawser around its smaller end, the slack of the
hawser is passed around the shaft of our patent winch — an
apparatus of cogs and levers standing in our bows — and everything in far less time than it has taken me to describe it, is
ready for *heaving*.

Then comes the hard work. The hawser is hauled *taut;*
the strain is increased; everybody, captain, cook, steward, and
doctor, is taking a *spell,* for dignity does not take care of
its hands in the middle pack; until at last, if the floes be
not too obdurate, they separate by the wedge action of our
bows, and we force our way into a little cleft, which is kept
open at either side by the vessel's beam. The ice which allows itself to be thus severed, is rare enough. Oftentimes we
heave, and haul, and sweat, and, after parting a ten-inch
hawser, go to bed wet, and tired, and discontented, with nothing but experience to pay for our toil. This is *warping*.

But let us suppose that, after many hours of this sort of
unprofitable labor, the floes release their pressure, or the ice
becomes frail and light. "Get ready the lines!" Out jumps
an unfortunate with a forty-pound hook upon his shoulder,
and plants his hook on a distant cape, in line with our wished-

for direction. The poor fellow has done more than carry his hook; for a long white cord has been securely fastened to it, which they *pay out* from aboard the ship. This is a whale-line — cordage thin, light, strong, and of the best material. It passes inboard through a block, and then, with a few artistic turns, around the capstan. Its slack is carried to a little windlass at our main-mast. Now comes the warping again. The first or heavy warping we call heaving; this last is a civilized perform-ance — all hands walking around with the capstan-bars to the click of its iron cogs, or else, if the watch be fresh, to a jolly chorus of sailors' songs.

We have made a few hundred yards of this light warping, when the floes, never at rest, open into a tortuous canal again. We can dispense with the slow traction of the capstan, and a party of human horses take us in tow. Each man — or horse, if you please — has a canvas strap passing over his shoulders and fastened to the tow-line. This harnessing is no slight com-fort to hands wet with water at the freezing point; and with its aid they tug along, sometimes at a weary walk, and some-times at a dog-trot. This is *tracking.*

When we could neither *heave,* nor *warp,* nor *track,* nor sail, we resorted to all sorts of useless expedients, such as sawing, cutting, and vainly striving to force our way into a more hope-ful neighborhood. It was long before experience taught us to spare ourselves this useless labor.

The men found it hard to await idly a change for better things. Yet for twenty-one days they were imprisoned, never leaving a little circle of some six miles' radius, and measuring their progress by yards and feet, rather than by miles.

A breeze, a steady breeze blowing hard for days, fresh-ened into a southeaster; soon broken floes were on all sides. Only too glad to be once more free, they bored through them, and, three weeks after attempting the Middle Passage, they were back where they had started, still faced with the need to get north of Melville Bay.

Less a bay than a large horseshoe indentation of the coast, it is exposed to the middle ice that intrudes upon its shores, pushed there by the prevailing northwest winds and kept there by the great ice harvest that streams out of Lancaster Sound. Through these ice-clogged waters the Baffin whalers made their annual attempt to pass; Kane grimly noted that since 1819, "from which we may date the opening of Melville Bay, no less than 210 vessels have been destroyed in attempting its passage."

Their entry into this region dreaded by whalers was ominous. It blew a gale. The offing was obscured by fog, noisy with the crash and sharp noises of the ice drifting by. Twice they were called to warp the ship out of an iceberg's path. "Imagine a mass as large as the Parthenon bearing down upon you before a storm-wind!" And the coast along which they sought anchorage was truly iron-bound: bergs, floes, and hummock ridges, "in all the disarray of wintry conflict, cemented in a basis of ice ten feet thick. It was the first time I had witnessed the stupendous results of ice action," Kane wrote.

Two days of warping and sailing, sailing and warping — a dreary routine — gained them forty miles; but already August, the last month of summer, was upon them. "Our prospects were far from cheery. The season of complete consolidation, when winter closes the navigation of these seas, could not be postponed beyond fifty days longer, and we had yet to double the ice of Melville." Days added up to weeks; their rate was painfully slow, their strenuous efforts monotonous and dull; but for Kane the days were shot through with many kinds of adventures.

There was always the ice to study, the ice in its many forms and moods and meanings. He watched a floe drive on the shore. "This assailing floe was three feet eight inches thick, perhaps a mile in diameter, and moving at the rate of a knot an hour. Its weight was some two or three millions of tons. So irresistible was its momentum that as it impinged against the solid margin of the land ice, there was no recoil, no interruption to its progress. The elastic material corrugated before the enormous pressure; then cracked, then crumbled, and at last rose, the lesser over the greater, sliding up in great inclined planes. This imposing process of dynamics is called *Hummocking*. Its most striking feature was its unswerving, unchecked, continuousness. Tables of white marble were thrust into the air as if by invisible machinery."

Or there were lessons to be learned watching the icebergs. "It was the motion of the floating bergs which first gave me the idea of a great undercurrent to the north. Their drift followed some system of advance entirely independent of the wind. While the surface ice or floe was moving southward with the wind, the bergs were making a northern progress, crushing through the floes in the very eye of the breeze at a measured rate of a mile and a half an hour."

The bergs themselves bore evidence of their glacial past; many were covered with detritus — quartz, gneiss, clay slate; and some bore unmistakable marks of the moraines through which they had passed.

And the animal life! The sleep-happy, ever alert seals, the bears chronically curious. And the rich bird life — immense flocks of the little auk crowded the margins of the floes to eat the plentiful plankton life of Northern waters; "like all birds feeding on crustacean life, they are very red in meat, juicy, fat, delicate, and flavorsome." While engrossed in eating, the birds were easily killed. "We shot enough of them, from the time of their arrival till we entered Lancaster Sound, to furnish the tables of all our messes abundantly." When they killed their first bear, Kane ate some of its liver to discredit those who claimed it was poisonous, and converted a skeptical crew to his views. Liver was "accepted afterwards as a frequent dish upon our breakfast table." Bear meat was strong and its flavor capricious. "One day he is quite beefy and bearable; another hircine, hippuric, and damnable. As part of my Polar practice, I make it a point — albeit I esteem a discriminating palate — to eat of everything. Seal is not fishy, but *sealy*, and sea-gull is worthy of all honorable mention."

Eating, observing, studying, warping and sailing, the men of the *Advance* moved toward the North Water. On August 18 the ship finally "bore across to the west in more open water than we had seen for several weeks." They were past the barrier, steering for Lancaster Sound.

One major difference between the Arctic and those parts of the world Kane had so far seen was the suspension of all concepts of day and night. At first it was a novelty to see the midnight Arctic sun set into sunrise, and pleasant to find the same unvarying daylight. It appealed to Kane's temperament that "no irksome night forced upon you its system of compulsory alternations. I could dine at midnight, sup at breakfast-time, and go to bed at noonday; and but for an apparatus of coils and cogs, called a watch, would have been no wiser and no worse. My feeling was at first an extravagant sense of undefined relief, of some vague restraint removed. I seemed to have thrown off the slavery of hours." But soon the perpetual light became garish and disturbing. Gradually he became aware of an unknown excitant, a stimulus, acting constantly, that robbed him of sleep and made his waking hours a blur of speeded-up activity. Kane, a child of the Temperate Zone, habituated to day and night, began to feel, "with more of emotion than a man writing for others likes to confess to, how admirable as a systematic law, is the alternation of day and night."

The weeks spent in the bay gave the expedition a brief, sorely needed schooling for the sterner conditions ahead. For even as they headed across and out of Baffin Bay, Kane knew that "it was now beyond doubt that we were to winter among the scenes of Arctic trial."

A gale, to whose perils were added fog and a mountainous coast toward which they were driving, blew the *Advance* south to Lancaster Sound. "About three o'clock in the morning of the twenty-first, another sail was reported ahead. When I reached the deck, we were nearly up to her. It was the *Felix*, commanded by that practical Arctic veteran, Sir John Ross [1777-1856]. I shall never forget the heartiness with which the hailing officer sang out, 'You and I are ahead of them all.' It was so indeed." Austin, whom they had missed at Disko, was with two of his ships at Pond Bay, while his other two ships were exploring the north side of Lancaster Sound; Captain Penny, commanding two ships which the *Advance* had met just two days before, was somewhere in the gale. "The *Felix* and the *Advance* were in the lead."

Kane was thrilled when a few minutes later the seventy-three-year-old Sir John Ross himself came on deck — now one of the heroes of the Arctic. The leader of two polar expeditions already, he had, in the second one, performed the unparalleled feat of wintering four years in Arctic snows. "And here he is again, in a flimsy cockle-shell, after contributing his purse and his influence, embarked himself in the crusade of search for a lost comrade." It was a crusade. Eleven ships in the same vicinity at almost the same time, bound on the same mission, directed to the same area. Lady Franklin's own ship, the *Prince Albert*, under the command of Captain Forsyth, came alongside the very next night.

During the next few weeks, when the ships met and parted and again met, there was visiting back and forth. Kane compared ships and equipment.

Westward the searching ships sailed — down Lancaster Sound; and as they sailed they poked into each bay and scrutinized every cliff and cape of its northern side. On Cape Riley, high and abrupt, they found cairns and sledge-track marks, but no written word. Franklin *had* passed that way; pieces of cloth and painted wood ruled out the possibility of an Eskimo encampment, and no other white party was known to have camped on that shore. To Captain Penny's men the traces spelled out tragedy: they saw in them notice that the Franklin ships had been wrecked and that this was the remains of a camp made by starving men hopefully retreating toward Baffin Bay. Kane rejected this. He based his argument on the teeming life all around. But whatever the implications spelled out by stones and cloth and wood, the searchers had picked up the lost scent; all pressed forward.

A narrow and capricious navigation gathered most of the ships within the same quarter of a mile. They did not come together "out of design, but under the irresistible guidance of the ice." Once together, however, the leaders met to coordinate their operations, allocating the directions for each party. Even as they were talking, a messenger was seen running over the ice. "The news he brought us was thrilling. 'Graves, Captain Penny! Graves! Franklin's winter quarters!' We were instantly in motion."

Running, scrambling over the loose and rugged slope, they came, after a weary walk, to the crest of the isthmus that connects Beechey "Island" to Devon Island. "Here, amid the sterile uniformity of snow and slate, were the head-boards of three graves, made after the old orthodox fashion of gravestones at home. The mounds which adjoined them were arranged with some pretensions to symmetry, coped and defended with limestone slabs." Stark, piously respectful, and sad, the names, the ages, and the death dates of the three young sailors who were laid to rest far from their homes — this and only this was written for the searchers to read.

Near this pathetic graveyard were signs of that first wintering. Most prominent was a deposit of more than six hundred cans, emptied of their preserved meat and filled with limestone pebbles, made ready perhaps to serve as ballast on boating expeditions. Strewn around were fragments of canvas and cordage, clothing and scraps of paper, odds and ends of brass work — "in a word, the numberless reliquiae of a winter resting place." Yet there was "not a written memorandum, or pointing cross, or even the vaguest intimation of the conditions or intentions of the party."

In the absence of message or sign, they were forced to deduce the direction Franklin had taken on leaving that first winter's camp. Again there were "the tracks of a sledge, clearly defined and unmistakable both as to character and direction. They pointed to the eastern shores of Wellington Sound," in the same general course as those sighted at Cape Riley. Again they would have to argue from theory, from hope or fear, from wish. Did they believe in the "open polar sea," in ice-free waters *north* of the icy barrier through which they had fought their way? Then the evidence pointed toward Wellington Channel as the route Franklin took. Did they despair of finding a waterway along the American coast? Again, that long-sought waterway must exist further north. Kane found it very clear "that a systematic reconnaissance was undertaken by Franklin of the upper waters of Wellington, and that it had for its object an exploration in that direction as soon as the ice would permit."

Kane, subscribing to the open polar sea theory, was convinced that a deep warm current moving northward, strong enough to send massive bergs against wind and drift, made an ice-free Arctic Ocean an inevitable conclusion.

De Haven and Kane piled conjecture on conjecture, they reasoned as to what Franklin would have done: "Let us suppose the season for renewed progress to be approaching; Franklin and his crews looking out anxiously from their narrow isthmus for the first openings of the ice. They come: a gale of wind has severed the pack, and the drift begins."

It was clear from Franklin's character he would press to the north, through the open lead that lay before him. The searchers were tempted "by the insidious openings to the north in Wellington Channel, to push on in the hope that some lucky chance might point us to an outlet beyond." Though they stood on the highest point on Beechey and saw no open water north or west, they sailed for Wellington Channel, hoping for an "insidious opening."

The few remaining days of August passed in fluttering efforts. By September 3 they had zigzagged and tacked until they saw the undelineated western coast of Wellington Channel. "The ice is tremendous, far ahead of anything we have met with. The thickness of the upraised tables is sometimes fourteen feet; and the hummocks are so ground and distorted by the rude attrition of the floes, that they rise up in cones like crushed sugar, some of them forty feet high." A northwest wind made them seek the shelter of an inlet; it protected them from the drift, the slow procession of great floes. So strong was the hope for an open polar sea that not once, when noting and describing these mighty ice formations, did Kane ask himself whence they came.

Already the young ice was three inches thick. Before them stretched a terrifying sight, "the drift plain of Wellington Channel, impacted with floes, hummocks, and broken bergs. Our situation might be regarded as an ugly one in some states of the wind, but for the solid main floe to the north of us. This projected from the cliff and formed a reliable breakwater."

Their sweet security of the past few days was shattered by a crash:

We rushed on deck just in time to see the solid floe to windward part in the middle, liberate itself from its attachment to the shore, and bear down upon us with the full energy of the storm. The *Rescue* was first caught, nipped astern, and lifted bodily out of water; fortunately she withstood the pressure, and rising till she snapped her cable, launched into open water, crushing the young ice before her. The *Advance*, by hard warping, drew a little closer to the cove and, a few minutes after, the ice drove by just clearing our stern. Com-

modore Austin's vessels were imprisoned in the moving fragments and carried helplessly past us. In a very little while they
were some four miles off.

That afternoon every man worked hard to cut up the
young ice, tow the pieces out into the current, and clear
enough space to free the ship. By morning they could hoist
the sails; by the next afternoon they "were beating to the
west in Lancaster Sound." Now they were forced to hug
the southern shore, for the young ice, glazing over the
sound, formed a "viscid sea of sludge and *thickly-benders,*
from the northern shore to the pack, a distance of at least
ten miles. This was mingled with the drift floes from Wellington Channel, and in them steaming away manfully"
were two of Austin's ships. The *Advance,* without benefit
of steam and with a wind dead ahead, was mortified "first
to see our pack-bound neighbors force themselves from
their prison and steam ahead dead in the wind's eye, and
next to be overhauled by Penny and passed by both his
brigs. We are now the last of all the searchers. We are
here on a single track but little wider than the Dela-
ware or Hudson. There is no getting out of it, for the shore
is on one side and the fixed ice close on the other."

They were without heat inside the brig; it was uncom-
fortably cold; and Kane — sealing himself within the
India-rubber curtains of his berth, with his lamp burning
— noticed, as he wrote his journal, that his thermometer
registered a freezing temperature.

Fast-moving, tense, decisive, the events of the next few
days are recorded vividly in Kane's journal.

September 10. Unaccountable, most unaccountable, the caprices of this ice-locked region! Here we are all together again, all anchored to the fast-ice off Griffith's Island. The way to the west completely shut out.

September 11. Snow covering the decks and carried by our clothes into our little cabin. We are still alongside of the fixed ice.

September 12. The heavy snow changed to a drifting drift. At three the *Rescue* parted her cable's hold and was carried out to sea, leaving two men, her boat, and her anchors behind. We snapped our stern cable, lost our anchor, swung out, but fortunately held by the forward line. I have seldom seen a night of greater trial. The wind roared over the snow floes and everything about the vessel froze into heavy ice. The *Rescue* was last seen beating to windward against the gale.

September 12. 10 P.M. Just from deck. How very dismal everything seems! The snow is driven like sand upon a level beach; the wind, too, is howling in a shrill minor, singing across the hummock ridges. The thermometer stands at 14°. At this temperature the young ice forms in spite of the increasing movement of the waves, stretching out from the bow in long, zigzag lines of smoothness resembling watered silk. Now when you remember that we are in open sea, attached to precarious ice, and surrounded by floating streams; that the coast is unknown and the ice forming inshore so as to make harbors, if we knew them, inaccessible, you may suppose our position is far from pleasant.

September 13. At about three this morning the squadron commenced getting under way. The rime-coated rigging was cleared; the hawsers thrashed; the ice-clogged boats hauled in; the steamers steamed, and off went the rest of us as we might. The *Rescue* is now the object of our search. Could she be found the captain has determined to turn his steps homeward. We are literally running for our lives, surrounded by the imminent hazards of sudden consolidation in an open sea. All minor perils, nips, bumps, and sunken bergs are discarded;

we are staggering along under full sail, forcing our way while we can.

Our captain who was at his usual post, conning the ship from the foretop-sail yard, made out the *Rescue,* and immediately determined upon boring the intervening ice. This was done successfully, the brig bearing the hard knocks nobly. We were no sooner through, than signal was made to the *Rescue* to "cast off," and our ensign was run up from the peak; the captain had determined upon attempting a return to the United States.

De Haven, whose virtuosity in ice navigation earned him the admiration of the British, was obeying his instructions — which urged that unless special circumstances warranted, he was to "endeavor not to be caught in the ice during the winter, but that he should, after completing his examination, make his escape." Kane could take no exception to his commander's decision; he could only comment that the officers of our little squadron felt "unmitigated regret that we were no longer to co-operate with our gallant associates under the sister flag."

But the *Rescue* was unworkable. She had had a frightful time: clogged with ice, short-handed, she had been forced to beat about until miraculously she succeeded in holding on to the land hummocks. Her rudder post had been split; the *Advance* took her in tow, and together the two headed east. At the thought that the actual search was finished, Kane felt no elation; it was "a saddened homeward bound for all of us."

However somber Kane's thoughts, however mixed his reactions — now wanting to stay, now fearful lest they be imprisoned in their inlet refuge — De Haven was only troubled by the thought he might have reached his decision too late. The low temperatures persisted and repeatedly they had to bore their way through the young ice. Night now gave them three hours of complete darkness. "It was danger to run on, yet equal danger to pause. Grim winter was following close upon our heels; and even the captain began to feel anxious."

Kane lay in his bunk. September 14 was a memorable day. It was close to zero, and he was trying to warm his stiffened limbs. He listened — the sound came clearly through the hull and filled his den — to the vessel's crunching her way through the new ice. The sound was not like the grinding of old, formed ice, nor like the slushy scraping of sludge. As he lay there, the noise, "grew less, then increased, then stopped, then went on again, but jerking and irregular; and then it waned, and waned, and waned away to silence. Down came the captain: 'Doctor, the ice has caught us: we are frozen up.' On went my furs at once. As I reached the deck, the wind was there, blowing stiff, and the sails were filled and puffing with it. It was not yet dark enough to hide the smooth surface of ice that filled the horizon, holding the American expedition in search of Sir John Franklin imbedded in its centre."

"There we are, literally frozen tight in the mid-channel of Wellington Straits."

V I

Winter:

Drifting with the Arctic Pack

Almost a month passed and the energetic explorers, their sails useless, had their first taste of a motionless ship. The ice dominated their lives. Unspoken but always present was a question: would the ice be their jailer, or a ruthless enemy intent on destroying those who dared invade its seat of authority?

Kane noticed, as the ice first clutched at them, that the region which but a week before had been teeming with animal life was now almost deserted. Sadly he enumerated the birds whose wings and cries had filled the air and the large blubber-coated animals of the sea, adding: "Whatever gave us life and incident, had vanished." Northward the ice drift carried them as the light waned and the cold increased.

Neither darkness nor freezing temperatures — mitigated only by a lard lamp in the cabin — distressed them as did the condensing moisture; sweat oozed from the beams and the bedding, and bunks looked as though they had been left out in a drizzle.

Northward they drifted, past Beechey Island, "the isthmus of the Graves," past their old landmarks, up Wellington Channel beyond anything recorded on the charts.
Other men and other ships had wintered in the Arctic,
but only once before had a ship passed a winter in the
pack itself and escaped intact.

In the weeks since the *Advance* had entered Lancaster
Sound, only three days had been free of gales that rose
and fell in alternating series. Kane remarked on the
men's adjustment to life under harrowing conditions:
"Creatures of habit, those who were anxious have forgotten their anxiety: glued fast here in a moving mass, we
eat, and drink, and sleep, unmindful of the morrow." He
added his own reaction to a night filled with such tense
dread that he slept in his clothes — he "dreamed of being
presented to Queen Victoria."

By September 22, "ice-cradled," they floated to the
upper, unknown stretches of Wellington Channel. Blessed
with a beautifully clear sky, they saw in the north a new
"wide channel leading to the westward. A dark, misty-
looking cloud which hung over it [technically termed
frost-smoke] was indicative of much open water in that
direction." To the channel, which appeared to lead to the
open sea, De Haven gave the name of Maury, "whose
theory with regard to an open sea to the north is likely to
be realized through this channel. To the large mass of
land visible between northwest to north-northeast, I gave
the name of Grinnell, in honor of the head and heart of

the man in whose philanthropic mind originated the idea of this expedition, and to whose munificence it owes its existence."

The next day was, in De Haven's dry understatement, uncomfortable. Kane had the first watch; he was "anxiously observing the ice; for I am no sailor, and in emergency can only wake my comrades." But his sharp eyes had noticed that disturbances of the ice floes were always preceded by specific noises that reminded him of "whining puppies and swarming bees," only shriller and more clamorous; that, shortly after, the vessel would start to tremble, "like an ague-fit, under the pressure." A partial breakup occurred that morning.

The *Advance* was heavily nipped between two floes; the weight of the ice, piled and tumbled on the deck, menaced the ship. "All hands are out, laboring with picks and crowbars to overturn the fragments that threaten to overwhelm us. Add to this darkness, snow, cold, and the absolute destitution of surrounding shores. This uprearing of the ice is not a slow work; it is progressive but not slow. . . . Impelled by this irresistible, bearing-down floe-monster, we crush, grind, *eat* our way, surrounded by the ruins of our progress. In fourteen minutes we changed our position 80 feet. Sometimes the ice cracks with violence, almost explosive throughout the entire length of the floe. Sometimes the hummock masses, piled up like crushed sugar around the ship, suddenly sink into the sea, and then fresh mounds take their place."

The upheaval left the ship on an uneven keel; one end was eighteen inches higher than the other! By the end of September, the rapidly increasing cold held out promise of a certain degree of security and stability. The men felt they were fixed for the winter. "We arranged our rude embankments of ice and snow around us, began to deposit our stores within them and got out our felt covering that was to serve as our winter roof."

With their snow storehouses finished, preparations for winter living began. Five tons of coal, passed up out of the hold, bucket by bucket, was piled on the ice; the small boats were taken from the deck and carefully placed close at hand alongside; the sails were covered and stacked. "Little had we calculated the caprices of Arctic ice. About ten o'clock A.M., a large crack opened."

Nothing warned them that worse was to follow. Two men were sent to the nearest shore to arrange a food depot and Kane, sighting a seal, went out to hunt. Suddenly at noon the signal to return to the ship was sounded. Kane, though out of earshot, had been warned by the *"humming of bees"* and hastened back. He had returned when, an hour later, "that unmistakable monitor, the *young puppies,"* began. The ice was breaking up in all directions — obedient to unseen pressures. All hands turned to, officers included, and the land party, returning at that moment tired and dinnerless, went to work with the rest. Before dark everything had been put back on board except the coal; and, so well did the crew work, of this they lost but a ton or two. This crisis provided instruction: it taught those who had not yet understood how capriciously insecure was their position. Not even after seventeen days of very low temperatures was the ice to be trusted.

Their housings still were not completed nor were there fires below; they were so liable to momentary and violent change that it would have been impracticable to put up stoves. The lard lamp in the cabin raised the temperature to the middle forties, a satisfactory climate for men already inured to acute cold; and, save for the condensed moisture that dripped from everything, they would have considered their arrangements comfortable. As a temporary measure, Kane placed canvas gutters around the hatchways; these collected several tin cans of water daily, water that otherwise would have been added to the slop on the cabin floor. The state of things "was on the whole, exceedingly comfortless, and, to those whom the scurvy had attacked, full of peril." Not until the middle of October were the stoves put up; and another month passed before the *Advance* was ready for the winter.

A housing of thick felt was drawn over the deck, resting on a sort of ridgepole running fore and aft, and coming close down on the sides. Rime and snowdrift quickly made it almost impervious to the weather. The cook's galley was under the main hatch, its stovepipe rising through the housing above, and a funnel-shaped apparatus for melting snow attached below. The bulkheads between cabin and forecastle were taken down and two stoves, one at each end of the berth deck, warmed officers and seamen alike. "We had, of course, a community of all manner of odors."

In October, the northward drift reversed itself and brought them back to Lancaster Sound.

Neither darkness nor cold kept Kane from hunting whenever possible. To secure seal, he adopted the Eskimo tactics of great patience and complete immobility; and, though he suffered sitting motionless for hours in the bitter cold, he was fascinated by his prey. "Very strange are these seals. A countenance between the dog and the mild African ape — an expression so like that of humanity, that it makes gun-murderers hesitate."

Scurvy and a craving for fresh meat steeled Kane's heart to the pathos of the dying seals. He felt he had been penalized for his deed when, on returning to the ship, he found one toe frostbitten; it was restored to its original vitality by snow-rubbing. (Frostbite was a common complaint. Ears were especially vulnerable and Kane, as medical officer, ordered the men to take off their earrings, "barbaric pendules, doubtless of bad gold, but good conducting power.")

During the month of November, pushed by winds or carried by currents, the ship oscillated in the region where Wellington Channel and Lancaster Sound are joined. Helpless among the floating masses, the men thought of the floe that carried them as a protection against the approaches of others, less friendly. As it became apparent that they would enter Lancaster Sound, their fears of being frozen in the pack gave way to a new fear: the dreaded prospect of a continuous drift. Their hope of staying stationary alongside a rigidly fixed land floe was gone.

Again and again Kane recorded the mighty movement of the pack, the heaving, rolling, surging, tottering, and falling of huge blocks; ice in movement filled the stillness of the Arctic night with a variety of sounds. "You heard the heavy *sough* of the snow-padding" as it received a twenty-ton block that toppled over; "but this was only the deep bass accompaniment to a wild, yet not unmusical chorus. There was the ringing clatter of ice made friable by the intense cold, the low whine which the ice gives out when we cut it at right angles with a sharp knife, rising sometimes to a shriek; the whirr of rapidly urged machinery; the hum of multitudes: and all these mingled with tones that have no analogy among the familiar ones of unadventurous life."

December brought its moments of imminent destruction. "Everything getting ready for the chance of a hurried good-by to our vessels. Pork, and sugar, and bread put up in small bags to fling on the ice. Every man his knapsack and change of clothing. Arms, bear-knives, ammunition out on deck and sledges loaded. Yet this thermometer, at −30°, tells us to stick to the ship while we can."

Excitement and anxiety alternated as the floe, driving like a race horse, threatened instant destruction. Cracks streaked across their floe, reducing its size; chasms opened and closed again with a sound like escaping steam. Everything indicated a crisis. Sledges, boats, packages of all sorts were placed in order, every man was at work, officer and seaman alike. "The *Rescue,* crippled and castaway from us on the further side of a chasm, was deserted, and her company consolidated with ours. Our own brig groaned and quivered under the pressure against her sides." The crisis prolonged itself for many tense days. "Nakedness of resources, even more than perpetual darkness and unendurable cold, makes our position one of bitterness."

Crisis upon crisis! Kane noted the men's reaction — "the sedative effect of a protracted series of hazards." When the brig, pushed to the crest of a floe, balanced so precariously that the boatswain called out for the men to "stand from under," an officer, knowing that the fires had not been put out and that if the stoves fell the stores still aboard would be burned, swung himself back on deck and rushed below. "He found two persons in the cabin; the officer who had been relieved from watch-duty a few minutes before, quietly seated at the mess-table, and the steward as quietly waiting on him. 'You are a meal ahead of me,' he said; 'you didn't think I was going out upon the ice without my dinner.' "

The *Advance* had been well chosen. The little brig remained unhurt despite the frantic pressure clutches of the ice, and Kane, impressed with a drift of one hundred and eleven miles in the first nineteen days of December, did not doubt that the ship would float into Baffin Bay. But the executive officer drilled the crew for an emergency. He repeatedly mustered them for an ice march with knapsacks on their backs, inspected every article, and ordered the provisions and stores packed snug, marked, and made ready. The openings and closings about their floe, dangerous, but too uniform to be exciting, added to the frequency of alarm and increased their proficiency.

Rehearsals for disaster provided an outlet for the fear that beset them: once on the ice, safe but shipless, with sledges and knapsacks, stores and provisions prepared and accounted for — then what? Happily, Captain De Haven was spared the necessity of deciding.

As Kane had responded to unending day, so now he was conscious of perpetual night. His journal carefully notes the moon's domination of the sky. "10 A.M. The day is clear; but the moonlight so confounds itself with the day as to make a merely solar register impossible. 11 A.M. Day upon us on one side, and the moon bright on the other: moonlight and sunlight blend overhead." Kane's medical eye was struck "with the bleached faces of my mess-mates. The sun left us finally only sixteen days ago; but for some time before he had been very chary of his effective rays; and our abiding-place below has a smoky atmosphere of lamplit uncomfortableness. No wonder we grow pale with such a cosmetic."

While waiting that moment which decreed the return of light, the resurge of health and hope, Kane used the dreary enforced leisure to tell "something about the cold in its sensible effects, and the way in which as sensible people we met it." He was struck first by "the freezing

up of our water-casks, the drip-candle appearance of the
bung-holes, and our inability to lay the tin cup down for
a five-minute's pause without having its contents made
solid. Next came the complete inability to drink without
manufacturing it. We had to quarry out the flinty, glassy
lumps, and then melt it in tins for our daily drink."

The effect of cold on their food supplies gave Kane the
chance to join his choicest scientific vocabulary to the style
of the tall tale. Their barrels of dried apples became
"one solid breccial mass of impacted angularities, a con-
glomerate of sliced chalcedony." Dried peaches the same.
"To get these out of the barrel, or the barrel out of them,
was impossible. We found, after many trials, that the
shortest and best plan was to cut up both fruit and barrel
by repeated blows with a heavy axe, taking the lumps below to thaw." Sauerkraut reminded him of "mica, or
rather talcose slate. A crow-bar with chiseled edge ex-
tracted the *laminae* badly; but it was perhaps the best
thing we could resort to." Their brown sugar, when
frozen, looked like cork raspings imbedded in liquid
gutta percha and then allowed to harden. "Extract with
the saw; nothing but the saw will suit. Butter and lard,
less changed, require a heavy cold chisel and mallet.
Flour undergoes but little change, and molasses can at
$-28°$ be half scooped, half cut by a stiff iron ladle. Pork
and beef are rare specimens of Florentine mosaic:
crow-bar and pick-axe! for at $-30°$ the axe can hardly
chip it."

He filled page after page with the ludicrous miseries of

their shipboard life. "We have two climates, hygrometri-
cally as well as thermometrically, at opposite ends of the
scale. A pocket-handerchief, pocketed below in the region
of our stoves, comes up unchanged. Go below again and it
becomes moist, flaccid and almost wet. Go on deck again,
and it resembles a shingle covered with linen. I could pick
my teeth with it." Kane cherished three personal luxuries
to remind him of better times — silk next to his skin, a
toothbrush for the teeth, and white linen for the nose.
"Everything else is Arctic and hairy — fur, fur, fur."

Not the perpetual cold, the everlasting sameness, nor
the self-imposed exile from the active world of their
brother men — none of these tried the men most. The effect of the permanent darkness was obvious. Faces had
a peculiar waxy paleness; eyes became recessed and
strangely clear. Everyone complained of shortness of
breath. Even the appetite changed: frozen ham fat and
sauerkraut swimming in olive oil were favorites without
the men's even being aware of a craving for the high-fat
content diet of the Arctic. External symptoms mirrored
the inroads made on morale. Men moped, became testy,
and more and more solaced themselves with fantasy. Before long Kane was dealing with the most feared of all
Arctic enemies — scurvy.

Kane's medical training, his observant, clinical eye, and
above all his response to empirical results, gave him an approach to its proper treatment. At first he used the standard regime of "strenuous and constant effort at washing,
diet, and exercise to keep the scurvy at bay." Little by

little the order and the importance of these three prophylactic elements changed.

Soon "pains in the joints, rheumatisms, coughs, loss of appetite, and general debility," extended over the whole company. "We are a ghastly set of pale faces, and none paler than myself. I find it a labor to carry my carbine." A month later the inroads made by scurvy became greater. "Old pains were renewed, old wounds opened; even old bruises and sprains, received at barely remembered periods, came to us like dreams."

The living space for thirty-three men, well and sick together, Kane noted ruefully, was less than the size of his father's library. In this cabin "three stoves and a cooking-galley, four Argand and three bear-fat lamps burn with the constancy of a vestal shrine. Damp furs, soiled woolens, cast-off boots, sick men, cookery, tobacco-smoke, and digestion are compounding their effluvia around and within me." A thermometer at the head of his cot gave a mean temperature of 64°, at his feet, +16° to −4°: "ice at my feet, vapor at my head."

December 22, a Sunday, was the "midnight of the year!" Christmas came and cheer with it: a play was given, special dishes served, presents exchanged and Kane, "to protect the mess from indigestion," prescribed two bottles of Cognac from the medical stores. Nevertheless the symptoms of scurvy among the crew still increased and became more general. "I long for the light," Kane exclaimed. "Dear, dear sun, no wonder you are worshiped!"

They celebrated the first day of 1851 with an extra dinner and a few bottles of wine; "but there was no joy in our merriment; we were weary of the night, as those who watch for the morning."

"Presently the sun came: never till the grave-sod of the ice covers me, may I forgo this blessing of blessings again! I looked at him thankfully with a great globus in my throat."

The twenty-ninth of January. After an absence of eighty-six days the sun was to reappear and the men, waiting and watching, stood ready to greet him with three cheers. Kane was in "no mood to join the sallow-visaged party. I took my gun, and walked over the ice about a mile away from the ship to a solitary spot, where a big hummock almost hemmed me in, opening only to the south." Soon from the ship he heard the shouts of the men and then, waiting until the completed "orb fluttered on the horizon," he fired his gun in salute. Only a moment the sun stood there. His shot signalized "the conjunction of sunrise, noonday, and sunset."

The floe on which the two brigs nested traveled the length of Lancaster Sound; and, when the great pack of which they were part, met and merged with the floes of Baffin Bay, it was subjected to Titanic pressures. Then fully launched in the bay, still attached to their floe, they drifted southward; they estimated they were following the American coast at some forty to seventy miles from land. They were on a wide, flat, ice-covered expanse; even icebergs, those monuments of power that had crowded the Greenland side, were absent.

There was little to do. Prisoners of the ice, they must wait for the sun to set them free. They were amazed to see the cold drop to new lows during February and March — for the first time the mercury congealed in the thermometers.

Cold as it was, only when a wind or drift storm kept them cooped up did they forgo their regular midday exercise. The effort was hard, and the active exercise, accompanied by pains in the joints, sometimes hardly bearable; yet they put in at least three hours a day. They played football, slid down hummocks, played tag, and leapfrog; they constructed a fine skating rink; they took long walks — anything to use muscles not otherwise taxed, anything to shake off the lethargy induced by their enforced inaction. It was part of Kane's drive against scurvy.

Scurvy, which seemed to wane for a time, returned with renewed and even exacerbated virulence. Old, forgotten injuries suddenly flared into active sores. De Haven suffered excruciating pain from a finger joint that a schoolmaster's ruler had hurt twenty-five years ago; and Kane's lance wound that had been healed for three years became abscessed "wherever it bore the marks of the surgeon's knife."

Some men refused to take the lime juice and sauerkraut Kane advised and clung to a diet of salt junk and hardtack, ship bread and beef. Kane converted the rejected delicacies into "an abominable doctor-stuff," appealing to their spirit of martyrdom. "Three times a day did these high-spirited fellows drink a wineglass of olive-oil and lime juice, followed by raw potato and sauerkraut, pounded with molasses into a damnable electuary. They ate nobly and got well." Kane was endlessly resourceful. When the supply of antiscorbutic drinks was exhausted, he manufactured a beer out of dried peaches and some raisins, using barley and brown sugar as a fermenting basis. "The men drank it in most liberal quantities."

The spring storms of March stirred the great pack to restlessness. Now the warning noises of the ice, the "young puppies" and the "humming of bees," made a happy melody that promised release. With returning light, Kane redoubled his efforts to get within shooting range of the seals who indulged their customary curiosity from a safe distance. Each day the conformation of the pack changed and he sought out the "beaches" where, from a five-foot shelf of dazzling ice, he looked below on water as black as a newly harrowed field. His trained hunter's eye anxiously scanned ice and water; he needed meat — fresh meat — for the invalids.

His responsibility as medical officer demanded this daily hunt. He knew from the Eskimo methods the craft required to secure a seal; but more than craft or skill was patience. Often the tantalizing sight of a seal would keep him "prostrate on the slushy ice for an hour and a half" — and he would suddenly see the animal disappear in the wake of a spouting whale before he had come within firing range.

Setting the pack in motion, the spring storms cracked the massive solidity into enormous pieces, the primary step leading to final dissolution. The storms warned the men to prepare for a new struggle with the ice fields and the abandoned *Rescue*, still lying close by, was made ready so that they would not be utterly dependent on the fate of the *Advance*. It was in good time. March ended with a regular gale. When the storm abated Kane found that a beach along which he had hunted "was swallowed up, crushed, crumbled, submerged, or uplifted in long ridges."

Not even in Lancaster Sound had the destruction of the ice surface been as certain. Then the intense cold and feeble winds of the late winter preserved the pack's integrity; now it was doubly attacked by the ever-lengthening days and the increased ferocity and frequency of the winds. Once again they saw icebergs cut a jagged line against the sky, and as before the water was filled with the great creatures of the Northern sea. Kane, standing at the edge of their diminished floe, saw narwhals "passing almost within reach." Seals, everywhere, were treading water with their horizontal tails "and the white whale was blowing purple sprays into the palpable sunshine."

Spring was coming to free them. By the middle of April they were able to put out their cabin lamps; henceforward they were "content with daylight, like the rest of the world." Having made the *Rescue* ready, the *Advance* was subjected to spring cleaning. Summer seemed very close at hand.

Each day brought a new, perilous excitement to Kane's daily hunting. Warm, bright, sunny days invited him to tramp for hours far from the ships, but the ice, soon to become floating rubbish, was already wet and crumbling. "The snow covered deceitfully some very dangerous cracks; in one of these I sunk neck deep. My carbine caught across it." Fortunately, a companion was there to pull him out. Or, investigating a cluster of small, cone-like elevations that pocked the flat, new ice formed by the previous night's cold over an open lead, he felt the ice vibrate. Presently, "in one concerted diapason, a group of narwhals, imprisoned by the congelation of the opening, spouted their release, scattering spray and snow in every direction." Fresh tracks warned him that he was not the undisputed hunter of that ice-covered ocean; the bear, "dependent upon his own predatory resources alone, and defying cold as well as hunger, guided by a superb instinct, confides himself to these solitary, unstable ice-fields."

"Never, in the warmest days of summer harvest-time, have I felt the heat so much as on this Arctic May-day," Kane wrote, but added that the sunshine wanted the sounds of summer — the silence was too complete. He also found the reflection from the snow excessive, and, like the men who were out with him, was stricken with snow blindness. For four agonizing days he found it impossible to write, and, what was more important for his scurvy patients, impossible to hunt. Nothing deterred

Kane for long from continuing his hunting efforts, however. His patients needed fresh meat and, though he was half-blind, the birds had returned, giving an assurance of food. "A filmy gauze floats between me and everything else. No sun, but a peculiar misty, opalescent glare. I bagged thirty-three auks; but my snow-blindness avenges them."

This, the characteristic disease of May, was severe and acute: it left some with disturbed, uncertain vision. Kane, always experimenting with ways to handle Arctic medical problems, approved of the Eskimo eye-shield — a disk of wood pierced by a horizontal slit. It afforded greater protection than "the colored goggles they had brought with them. The increased sensibility of the retina seemed to require a diminution of the quantity rather than a modification of the character of the ray."

Land! The cry was raised on May 19. Land it was — far distant, shadowy, high, snow-covered and strange. The next day gave them a complete range of dreary, snow-covered hills. But to eyes that had seen no land in the ninety-nine days since they looked on the Lancaster Sound headlands, the solid certainty of the glimpsed mountain ridges was inexpressibly gratifying. During May they drifted almost two hundred miles. "For the last four days of the month we were at the margin of the Arctic Circle, alternating within and without it. . . . We were experiencing at this time the rapid transition of seasons which characterizes this climate." The month pleasantly closed on them without adventure, but its last ten days were full of monitory changes.

The comparative safety in which the pack moved through broad reaches of Baffin Bay was threatened by the approaching congestion of Davis Strait. It was useless to speculate or plan the future. "We were the illustration of powerless ignorance; what we hoped for one day, we congratulated ourselves that we had escaped the next. We were rotating on the disk of a great wheel, with a ragged and constantly changing periphery."

June brought greater warmth. The snow-birds increased in numbers. The close presence of open water was seen in the trench alongside the ship. "The floating scum of rubbish advances and recedes with a regularity that can only be due to some equable undulation from without." A fog surrounded them, and, when it lifted, from a high nearby hummock they saw — not too distant — open water. "It seems like our cup of Tantalus; we are never to reach it. And while we are floating close upon it, the season is advancing; and if we are ever to aid our brothers in the search, we should even now be hurrying back."

"THE BREAK-UP AT LAST!" Thus in bold letters Kane spelled out the great event of June 5. It began with the warning cry: "She's breaking out: all hands aboard!" And within ten minutes every man scrambled toward his little Ark. They had to work and work fast. "The floe had been to us terra firma so long that we had applied to it all the purposes of land. Clothes and clothes-lines, sledges, preserved meats, kindling wood and planking, were now all bundled on board." Soon the intense activity was over; they stood on deck, looking at the floe. "We had the strange spectacle of an undulating solidity, a propagated wave borne in swell-like ridges, as if our ice was a carpet shaken by Titans." A sublime spectacle! To men who long had known an ice as firm as land, this sudden fluidity had the impact of an earthquake. Everything that for so long had been permanent was in flux.

Sailors again, the impatient men saw that only one cake of ice remained rigid and intact: a solid mass more than twenty-five feet thick tenaciously held the stern of the *Advance* cradled and upended. They tried to break it apart; it defied even an ingenious attempt to use another floe as a battering ram and the strong swells as power.

To free their ship they made sail, hoping the fresh steady wind would tear them loose. They knew that once unencumbered a few hours would see them in comparatively open water. "Our rate is ten feet per hour! Remember that the old man of Sinbad still clings to us, and that we carry the burden in this slow progress."

It was three days before they were "once more floating ship-fashion, in a ship's element." For hours they bumped and bored and warped, and then ran into an impenetrable ice fog. For safety they tied to a heavy floe. From it they obtained "fresh *thawed* water. This is the first time since the 15th of September that I have drunk water liquefied without fire. Eight months and twenty-four days; think of that, dear strawberry and cream eating family!"

Thus ended their nine-month besetment and their thousand-mile drift.

Running for the Greenland shore through a sea studded with a fanciful archipelago of low bergs and water-washed floes was uncomfortable. De Haven decided to refresh and restock at Whalefish Islands, then hasten back to Melville Bay and the north water, Lancaster Sound and Wellington Channel.

As Kane watched the men eagerly devour a seal, he "had reason to fear that we should not be able to resume our search effectively until the health of our party had undergone a tedious renovation."

Whalefish Islands revived memories of the previous year. "There were the same majestic fleets of bergs, the same legions of birds of the same varieties, the same anxious lookout, and rapid conning, and fearless encounter of ice-fields." On June 16 they were off the well-remembered cliffs. Again the Eskimos crowded the rocks, the dogs barked, and the children yelled. "A few lusty pulls and after nine months of drift, and toil, and scurvy, we were once more on terra firma."

From the Eskimos the men of the *Advance* learned that the winter was counted severe; according to the native calendar the season lagged, the birds had not started to breed.

At the Danish settlement, the crews enjoyed a five-day rest. They ate huge amounts of eider duck and codfish and chewed bitter herbs of every sort, they drank copiously of beer and danced the polka and the pee-oo-too-ka with the natives.

On the twenty-second they headed north. The weather was soft and delightful. Kane basked on deck all night, sleeping in the sun. Again they were in waters frequented by whalers. The first they met were two English ships. Their crews listened eagerly, wordlessly, while the men of the *Advance* told of their miraculous escape from the pack. "These burned children dread the fire; and their conversation opened our eyes to dangers we had gone through half-unconsciously." From them they received "newspapers, potatoes, turnips, eggs, and fresh beef enough to eat out every taint of scurvy. They took letters from us for home and cheered ship when we parted." Then they met a brig out of New London, "the bearer to us of letters and papers from home." Finally they caught up with the fleet itself, lying at the ice barrier, waiting to cross to the western coast. Again they were showered with luxuries — malt and brandy, vegetables and fresh quarters of beef, haunches of venison, and baskets filled with fresh eider eggs.

A few days later they hailed the small, ninety-ton *Prince Albert,* the only ship sent out in 1851 to continue the search for Franklin. On this trip it was commanded by William Kennedy, a warm-hearted man, half-Canadian, half-Indian. Kennedy's lack of nautical experience was balanced by years spent with the Hudson's Bay Company and the skill of his second in command, Joseph René Bellot, a young officer trained in the French Navy. Both were

volunteers, and they, with their handpicked crew of Shet-
landers, exemplified the internationalism and idealism
that characterized those who sailed on the Franklin
Search. Dedication to a common cause also made them
brothers to the Americans, and De Haven and Kennedy
decided to keep the three little ships together as a fleet.

"We followed each other's leads, warped, tracked, and
bored, and had all our conflicts with the ice together.
When we were beset and at a standstill, we enjoyed each
other's company, ate pemmican and loon, went out hunting, and took long walks with each other." The *Prince Albert* had received the present of an organ from the man
in whose honor the ship was named, and Kane heard
"The Garb of Old Gael" played as the ships lay in the ice
waiting to sail.

From the middle of July to the middle of August they
waited, impatient of the delays which every day forced on
them, making at most thirty-seven miles. Less than four
weeks remained to find a way out of the water where the
ice had trapped them, press north to Lancaster Sound,
complete their exploration of Wellington Channel and
return. The parties separated. The *Prince Albert* pushed
through and went on to a winter's work where Bellot's
sharp eyes found the strait named for him.

The *Advance* and the *Rescue* also escaped from a bay
rimmed with deadly bergs. It was August 19. "Our commodore has resolved on immediate return to the United
States. The game has been fairly played out. Lancaster
Sound was out of the question; and for our scurvy-riddled

crew, a nine months' winter in the ice of North Baffin would have been disastrous." Sailing southward, they found the waters entirely free from ice.

Kane closed the end of his account of this First Grinnell Expedition: "We left the settlements of Baffin Bay on the 6th of September, 1851, grateful exceedingly to the kind-hearted officers of the Danish posts; and after a run of some twenty-four days, unmarked by incident, touched our native soil again at New York. Our noble friend, Henry Grinnell, was the first to welcome us on the pier-head."

A sixteen-month voyage was ended.

The Book and the Expedition

THE FIRST GRINNELL EXPEDITION had introduced Kane to the Arctic. Knowledge of this world, with its terrors and its bounties, he shared with those whose livelihood depended on Northern whale fishing.

Now, back home, Kane had a story to tell. He wanted public sentiment to support a second, a private expedition for search and exploration; he wanted to present the Northern regions to his countrymen; and, as scientist, he wanted to detail the rewards and dangers faced by the Northern pioneers of the seafaring frontier.

September, 1851, was a dark moment for Lady Jane Franklin and the search. As De Haven brought his ships back, so back came the ships commanded by Penny, by Austin, and by Ross; the armada that had gone hopefully westward down Lancaster Sound and north up Wellington Channel slipped into home ports. They had failed in their mission. The graves and relics found on Beechey Island proved only the site of Franklin's first wintering.

The rescuers knew neither the direction the *Erebus* and *Terror* had taken nor the condition of the party.

The Admiralty's instructions to Sir John urged him to seek the Northwest Passage along waterways *to the south-west of Cape Walker;* only if that way was sealed off by ice was he to try a northern passage by way of Wellington Channel. Although Lady Jane Franklin "was not yet an Arctic authority she was an authority on Sir John and she knew that wherever his orders were to go, there he would go though it killed him." Twice out of her own funds she sent out the *Prince Albert,* twice she gave orders, first to Forsyth, then to Kennedy, directing the searchers southward toward King William Land; both times her orders were but half-heartedly carried out. It was hard for these men to turn southward into Peel Sound when the majority of Arctic experts insisted that all evidence pointed toward the north. Because the waters north of Lancaster Sound had barely been probed, geographers like Augustus Petermann and Matthew Maury could still postulate the open polar sea theory.

This beguiling theory seemed thoroughly compatible with Kane's first-hand knowledge of the rich animal life in the northerly polar waters. Theory and fact forged an argument that permitted him to believe that, even though six years had passed since the *Erebus* and *Terror* had sailed, some — he hoped many — men could have survived. Had not Sir John Ross spent four winters in the Arctic with but three fatalities? Kane knew a prolonged

stay in the Arctic was difficult but not impossible. And as
if to bolster up the waning hope of survivors, a whaling
captain suddenly recalled that Franklin had told him he
had augmented his supplies with enough food for seven
years!

Theory, facts, rumor, hearsay, were aired and examined by a stream of anonymous articles and letters fed to
the press by Lady Jane, exhorting Americans to further
efforts.

Against this background Kane sat down to write his account. De Haven quickly made his brief covering report
to the Secretary of the Navy, but Kane, writing for the
widest possible public, spent months on his book.

Authorship was unexpectedly trying. The bodily restraint imposed on Kane, a tireless walker and hunter,
was sudden and severe. He was merciless in his demands on his nature and physical strength. He drove himself, leaving his desk only to fill lecture engagements.
Hundreds of people in the principal Eastern cities came
to hear him. They saw a frail, small-boned man; they felt
that he was reserved, not shy, that he seemed absorbed,
not reticent; they enjoyed his odd quiet humor and original insight, and were amazed that a gentle scholar was a
doughty man of action.

Listening to his argument, they understood how he applied the advantages science and civilization put at his dis-
posal to lessons learned from the whaler and Eskimo to
create a way of living and working within the Arctic.

The rhythm of his speech was direct, staccato, colorful — different from the measured, balanced phrases in which he wrote. A recorded conversation of Kane's gives the sharpness and flavor of his speech; it adds a memorable scene not mentioned elsewhere. Asked for an instance of the "soul's power over the body," Kane paused, considered, and then suddenly spoke, the words seeming to spring out of him. "The soul can lift the body out of its boots, sir." (Was Kane summarizing his own fierce will to live?) "When our captain was dying — I say dying: I have seen scurvy enough to know — every old sore in his body was a running ulcer. I never saw a case so bad that either lived or died. There was trouble aboard: there might be mutiny. So soon as the breath was out of his body we might be at each other's throats. I felt that he owed even the repose of dying to the service. I went down to his bunk, and shouted in his ear, 'Munity, captain! mutiny!' He shook off the cadaveric stupor: 'Set me up,' said he, 'and order those fellows before me.' He heard the complaint, ordered punishment, and from that hour convalesced! Keep that man awake with danger, and he wouldn't die of anything till his duty was done."

But the book over which Kane fussed and labored held only second place in his thoughts. His lectures and a voluminous correspondence were directed to raising funds for an expedition the following spring. He exchanged letters with Lady Jane Franklin and her niece, Sophia Cracroft, one of the most indefatigible and prolific letter-writing teams of all time; with Henry Grinnell, and with

the Arctic friends he had met in the ice of Melville Bay.
As late as the beginning of May (1852) he still hoped to
join in that year's effort. His resolve to continue the search
was abiding and strong. Equally strong were his ideas
about the nature of the expedition; it should be under
private rather than navy auspices.

But Kane did not sail with the rescue parties of 1852.
His strenuous efforts had not succeeded and his book was
not finished. Disappointment added to overwork threatened to bring on an attack. Of what? A friend who saw
him at that time mentions Kane's "terribly intense" labors, says "his nervous system broke up," and adds "he ap-
prehended an attack of apoplexy, paralysis, or some other
form of cerebral explosion." Kane had a marked disposi-
tion to rely on hysteria when confronted with certain
kinds of frustrations. These seizures had overtones very
different from his bouts with rheumatism, scurvy, and assorted fevers; they were outlets for terrifying emotional
crises. Perhaps it was Kane's way of dealing with obstacles
which interposed themselves between his powerful urge
to achieve nobly and his certain knowledge that the time
allotted him was brief.

Was this attack prevented by "a more generous system
of living, and some relaxation of toil in book-making," or
did it evaporate before the actual presence of death?
It was then that fifteen-year-old Willie, his youngest
brother, took ill. Kane was his nurse and bedside companion until, in the last week of August, the boy died.
Sadly the summer slipped away; autumn softened the

family's grief. Kane "sprang to work again. The Book, the Book, and the Expedition, — only postponed, not abandoned, — engaged him."

Nothing seemed worth living for but to have one's name on the Arctic map, remarked Alfred Tennyson, Franklin's nephew; he might have been speaking of Kane, who was planning to search for Franklin along the shores of the open polar sea, an area approached by way of Wellington Channel. In his efforts to find adequate support, he encountered the happy windfalls and cruelly protracted refusals common to such ventures. Joseph Henry, Alexander Bache, and Matthew Maury, three eminent scientists, directors of the Smithsonian Institution, the Coast Survey, and the National Observatory, recommended him highly. Thus armed, Kane sought an interview with John P. Kennedy, then Secretary of the Navy. Kennedy, a well-known novelist and man of imagination, responded to Kane and to the mission. He ordered Kane on special duty and so raised his pay to "duty-rate"; ten volunteers from the navy were attached to his service — on navy pay; and medical supplies, rations, and valuable scientific equipment were furnished. In Grinnell, Kane found another stanch friend. The *Advance* was placed at Kane's service, and again made ready for a prolonged stay in the North.

In Kane's search for support for this first private expedition sent out from the United States, certain precedents were established. Kane was partially assisted by the government, partially by single wealthy backers — Grinnell, and George Peabody, whom Lady Franklin was to thank for his "munificent benevolence towards our English poor" — and partially by donations from scientific societies: the American Philosophical Society, the newly formed Geographical Society of New York, and others. Despite this help, a sizable sum remained to be raised by Kane himself. For twenty months he worked to that end.

In addition to donating his own pay, he lectured. Capturing an audience was serious business and highly competitive. He wrote Grinnell, who was acting as treasurer, that "every day is the scene of some rival attraction, and I have to do all I can to distance my rivals — Blitz [a magician and ventriloquist], Alboni [a famous contralto and a pupil of Rossini], and Emerson: we are all of one feather. No matter: so that I get my money, I do not care."

Physician, scientist, traveler, explorer — now Kane became businessman and administrator. A mountain of letters was written during the months of preparation; their "foresight, provident care, and thoughtful solicitude and labor would do honor to the head and all the hands of the Commissary Department of the Navy." Kane was minutely preoccupied with each aspect of the equipment and supplies. Pages filled with memoranda and calculations worked out the necessities that would be required by eighteen men engaged for two years in exploration of the Arctic; Kane arranged and rearranged the items in their order of importance — and cost.

His very limited funds made each purchase uncertain.

Did he order special guns so as to insure their performance in the field? The order had to be canceled because, as he said, "I hate to borrow a gun." He offered to go to New York to supervise the preparation of the pemmican required for the voyage, because "we could prepare it more economically and it would be of more certain quality." He went to Washington, rummaged around the Medical Department, and "succeeded in begging some $2000 worth of outfit." Only the essentials concerned him — but of these he had to be sure. "No one knows as well as an Arctic voyager the value of foresight," he wrote, adding that his equipment was simple, his provisions chosen with little regard for luxuries, his wardrobe moderate, and his supply of barter-goods adequate.

In contrast to this Spartan provisioning, the expedition had "a large, well-chosen library, and a valuable set of instruments for scientific observations." Kane had experienced the terrible tedium of the long polar night when he had lectured on "popular science, the atmosphere, the barometer, &c to the crew." He knew they were "not a very intellectual audience," but he remembered that they listened "with apparent interest and expressed themselves gratefully." Books provided sustenance for the mind and spirit. He also felt it imperative to collect data to further scientific studies of Arctic conditions.

Word that Captain E. A. Inglefield had penetrated Smith Sound and sighted open water beyond reached Kane in the early winter. The news galvanized him to still greater activity. Smith Sound suddenly became preferable

to Wellington Channel as the route to the open polar sea.
A few weeks later (December 14, 1852), addressing the
Geographical and Statistical Society, he disclosed his plan.
Skillfully blending together an assortment of motives to
make a potent appeal, he sounded the compelling theme
of quest — the hope of finding Franklin, of reaching the
North Pole, of sailing the Northwest Passage. With the
hope of all the searches which stirred men, the pressing
and pathetic, the traditional and noble and esoteric —
with these images he boldly filled the ears and minds of
his audience:

"The North Polar Ocean is a great mediterranean,
draining the northern slopes of three continents." There
Sir John Franklin and his followers had been lost for
seven years and the quickest hope for rescue was by the
most direct avenue — Smith Sound. In addition Smith
Sound offered certain well-founded advantages. And then,
by brilliant analogy and the logic of geography, Kane
deduced the far northern extension of Greenland. He
maintained that a land mass as a base of operations would
obviate "the capricious character of ice travel," its rich animal life would "sustain traveling parties," and its Eskimo
groups "still further along the coast" would be helpful to
the explorers.

Subtly mixing the known and the fancied, the factual
and the projected, the practical and the theoretical, Kane
led his audience to a conclusion that was an invitation to
voyage to the very top of the world. "It is my intention to

cover each sledge with a gutta percha boat, a contrivance which the experience of the English has shown to be perfectly portable. Thus equipped, we follow the trend of the coast, seeking the *open sea*. Once there, if such a reward awaits us, we launch our little boats, and, bidding God speed us, embark upon its waters."

The Smith Sound route! Its possibilities had been disclosed by Inglefield, its potentials had been grasped by Kane. Later events added a unique note to Arctic exploration: Smith Sound became a course on which was run the race for the "farthest north" record, the race to see which nation would first plant its flag at the Pole.

On February 26, long enough for his speech to be reported in England and have an effect, Kane, too ill to write, dictated a letter to Kennedy. He was alarmed! "The British Admiralty have adopted my scheme of search, and are about to prosecute it with the aid of steam. Nothing is left me, therefore, but a competition with the odds against me; and for this, even, I must hasten the preparations for my departure."

Ten days later, acknowledging Grinnell's notice that the *Advance* was in dock, he wrote: "The only means by which we can compete with the screw-steamer of Inglefield is by an early presence in Melville Bay, which may enable us to enter the North Water with the whaling-fleet by the June passage. My own impression as to Smith Sound is that it is seldom open until late in the summer — say last of August — unless the winter be what is termed an open one. I am discouraged. Should the ice be *fast* across the Sound, and my plan of sledge and boat progress come regularly into play, I ask no favors: steamer or no steamer, we shall do well."

A frantic rush possessed him during the weeks prior to departure. On May 30, 1853, the *Advance*, Elisha Kent Kane commanding the Second United States Grinnell Expedition, sailed out of New York Harbor bound for Smith Sound and the open polar sea. Though ten of the crew belonged to the navy, they with the others were selected for the voyage; all served "at salaries entirely disproportionate to their services; all were volunteers." In this expedition Kane dispensed with naval regulations and substituted three binding rules of conduct, announced beforehand and adhered to afterward. "These included — first, absolute subordination to the officer in command or his delegate; second, abstinence from all intoxicating liquors, except when dispensed by special order; third, the habitual disuse of profane language. We had no other laws."

Kane's last word was not of Inglefield and the race between them, nor of his health. As he was about to enter the fearful passage of Melville Bay, he wrote his brother Thomas "a brother's letter of confidence":

It is the quiet hour at which you and I begin to live; lacking midnight not overmuch, yet in a full glare of day.

Now that the thing — the dream — has concentrated itself into a grim, practical reality, it is not egotism, but duty, to talk of myself and my plans: I represent other lives and other interests than my own. The object of my journey is the search after Sir John Franklin: neither science nor the vain glory of attaining an unreached *North* shall divert me from this one conscientious aim.

V I I I

To the Open Polar Sea

HEADING NORTH for Greenland and Davis Strait, Kane knew he was following a path blazed by great pioneers. Before, when the *Advance* had drifted southward with the pack, he wrote: "We have passed, by the inevitable coercion of the ice, from the highest regions of Arctic exploration, the lands of Parry, and Ross, and Franklin, to the lowest, the seats of the early search for Cathay, the lands of Cabot, and Davis, and Hudson — all seekers after shadows. Men still seek Cathay!"

The *Advance*'s progress up the Greenland coast was not a repetition of her first voyage. Kane had business to transact and speed to make. He was racing against Inglefield — only on his return did he learn that the Englishmen had not sailed for Smith Sound. "I see two hundred and sixteen icebergs floating in a sea as dead and oily as the Lake of Tiberias," he wrote his father from Upernavik, the northernmost settlement. "The last week has been spent by me almost constantly in an open boat, striving to overcome the delays of an everlasting calm by making purchases without coming to anchor."

No longer a novice, authority and sureness stamped Kane's actions. He had outlined the advantages of sledging journeys — for that he needed dogs; he had proposed hunting as the best way to sustain the party — and for that he must have a hunter experienced in Eskimo techniques. The dog was the camel of these snow deserts; and "no Arab could part with him more grudgingly than do these Esquimaux. Congratulate me; for I have *all my dogs,* and the tough thews of the scoundrels shall be sinews of war to me in my ice-battles."

The dogs would have to be fed, and Kane knew his limited provisions were inadequate. The Danish superintendent recommended Hans Christian as an expert with the kayak and javelin. Kane hired the fat, good-natured boy of nineteen, who had demonstrated "his quality by spearing a bird on the wing." In addition to modest wages, Kane agreed to leave a "couple of barrels of bread and fifty-two pounds of pork with his mother; and I became munificent in his eyes when I added the gift of a rifle and a new kayak. We found him very useful; our dogs required his services as a caterer, and our own table was more than once dependent on his energies." In providing his expedition with dogs and a native hunter, Kane established a precedent all American explorers followed.

On August 3 the brig cleared Melville Bay and "its myriads of discouragements. The North Water, our highway to Smith's Sound, is fairly ahead." By the sixth, Cape Alexander and Cape Isabella, the headlands of Smith Sound, the Arctic's Pillars of Hercules, were in sight. "Whatever it may have been when Captain Inglefield saw it a year ago, the aspect of this coast is now most uninviting. As we look far off to the west, the snow comes down with heavy uniformity to the water's edge, and . . . on the right we have an array of cliffs." Rising sheer from the water, some eight hundred feet high, "they look down on us as if they challenged our right to pass." With Cape Alexander behind, they approached Littleton Island; nearby was the last headland "positively-determined" by Captain Inglefield. "We are fairly inside Smith Sound." But looking at the sky ahead which like a mirror reflected the dark of open water or the white of ice, Kane saw the light, the ominous iceblink.

On Littleton Island, Kane erected a cairn and, with an eye to future emergency, deposited a supply of stores and a lifeboat. "We placed along her gunwale the heaviest rocks we could handle, and, filling up the interstices with smaller stones and sods and moss, poured sand and water among the layers. This, frozen at once into a solid mass, might be hard enough, we hoped, to resist the claws of the polar bears."

While building this cache at Lifeboat Cove, they found evidence of human habitation. A few ruined walls here and there were all that spoke of a rude settlement. Ancient, but well preserved, it was impossible to estimate when the site had been abandoned.

The iceblink, seen from Flagstaff Point on Littleton Island, warned Kane what to expect. Within a few hours they "closed with ice to the westward. It was in the form of a pack, very heavy, and several seasons old." Soon he had need of all the lessons he had learned in ice navigation, but it was a profitless conflict, and he was grateful for the sheltered calm of "Refuge Harbor."

Among their "little miseries" were the fifty dogs. "To feed this family, upon whose strength our progress and success depend, is really a difficult matter." Two bears lasted but eight days; Kane saw that "the meagre allowance of two pounds of raw flesh every other day is an almost impossible necessity. Only yesterday they were ready to eat the caboose up, for I would not give them pemmican. Corn meal or beans, which Penny's dogs [not Eskimo dogs] fed on they disdain to touch; and salt junk would kill them." Smith Sound teemed with walrus, and to feed the dogs Kane went hunting. Though within twenty paces, his "rifle-balls reverberated from their hides like cork pellets from a pop-gun target, and we could not get within harpoon distance of one." Fortunately, one of the men found a dead narwhal, "a happy discovery, which secured for us at least six hundred pounds of good fetid wholesome flesh. We built a fire on the rocks and melted down his blubber: he will yield readily two barrels of oil."

The state of ice was Kane's major concern — no "ice-heaval has ever been described equal to this." Before him was a "melancholy extent of impacted drift, stretching as far as the eye could reach." Their efforts to work seaward through the floes all ended in failure. "We found ourselves at the end of the day's struggle close to the same imperfectly-defined headland which I have marked on the chart as Cape Cornelius Grinnell." He tried the only course left him, to follow the coastline. If the *Advance* could take the punishment of frequent groundings, the shoal water would protect her from the heavy ice. It was dreadfully slow work and Kane was reminded he had "no great time to spare; the young ice forms rapidly in quiet spots during the entire twenty-four hours." A change of weather and his own need for speed tempted him to forsake the shelter for another bout with the ice. His immediate objective was a low, rocky island, close to shore, about a mile ahead: "Godsend Ledge," it was called.

"*Midnight:* We did reach it; and just in time. At 11:30 P.M. our first whale-line was made fast to the rocks. Ten minutes later the breeze freshened, and so directly in our teeth that we could not have gained our mooring-ground." For two days the gale blew, and when the wind died down the ice outside closed steadily. "And here, for all I can see, we must hang on for the winter, unless Providence send us a smart ice-shattering breeze to open a road for us to the northward."

While waiting Kane had another fracas with the dogs. It was "worse than a street of Constantinople emptied upon our decks; the unruly, thieving, wild-beast pack!" Certainly he had not imagined such a state of things when he contemplated bringing them. Between the bed-lam on the ship and the unpromising ice of Smith Sound, Kane's only enjoyment was watching the antics of the walrus, as they came close to the brig, "shaking their grim wet fronts and mowing with their tusks the sea ripples."

The presence of those sphinx-faced monsters close to shore was said to be portent of a storm. The sky looked sinister; "a sort of scowl overhangs the blink under the great brow of clouds to the southwest." He could only wish for a better shelter in which to wait out the gale. "We had seen it coming, and were ready with three good hawsers out ahead, and all things snug on board."

The sequence of the next hours tested the ship and crew. The wind "came on heavier and heavier, and the ice began to drive more wildly."

Taking advantage of a momentary lull to rest and get dry, Kane, in his bunk, heard the sharp twanging snap of a cord: "Our six-inch hawser had parted, and we were swinging by the two others; the gale roaring like a lion to the southward.

"Half a minute more, and 'twang, twang!' came a second report. I knew it was the whale-line by the shrillness of the ring. Our noble ten-inch manila still held on." He hurried his last sock into its sealskin boot.

The manila cable was proving its excellence when I reached the deck. We could hear its deep Aeolian chant, swelling through all the rattle of the running-gear and moaning of the shrouds. It was the death song! The strands gave way with the noise of a shotted gun; and in the smoke that followed their recoil, we were dragged out by the wild ice, at its mercy.

We steadied and did some petty warping, and got the brig a
good bed in the rushing drift; but it all came to nothing.

There was but one thing left for us — to keep in some sort
of command of the helm, by going freely where we must
otherwise be driven. We allowed her to scud under a reefed
foretopsail; all hands watching the enemy, as we closed, in
silence. At seven in the morning, we were close upon the piling
masses. We dropped our heaviest anchor with the desperate
hope of winding the brig; but there was no withstanding the
ice-torrent that followed us. We had only time to fasten a
spar as a buoy to the chain, and let her slip. I had seen such
ice only once before, and never in such rapid motion. One
upturned mass rose above our gunwale, smashing in our bulwarks, and depositing half a ton of ice in a lump upon our
decks. Our staunch little brig bore herself through all this
wild adventure as if she had a charmed life.

Just then, their weighted ship was threatened by a low
water-washed berg which came driving straight at them.
Kane remembered a close escape in Melville Bay and, as
the berg moved close alongside, ordered an anchor planted
in its slope. It was an anxious moment: "Our noble tow-
horse, whiter than the pale horse that seemed to be pursu-
ing us, hauled us bravely on; the spray dashing over his
windward flanks, and his forehead ploughing up the lesser
ice as if in scorn." Dragged thus along a channel, they
finally found themselves under the lee of a berg, in a
comparatively open lead. "Never did heart-tried men
acknowledge with more gratitude their merciful deliver-
ance from a wretched death."

The day with its full share of trials passed; but more
was to come. Hardly did the men turn in to snatch a little
precarious sleep when the ice began to nip the *Advance*.

The brig bore the first shock well; after a moment of old-fashioned suspense, it rose by jerks above the thrusting ice. The next nip came from a veteran floe, twenty feet thick. "No wood or iron could stand this; but the shoreward face of our iceberg happened to present an inclined plane, descending deep into the water; and up this the brig was driven, as if some great steam screwpower was forcing her into a dry dock."

There seemed no way to keep the *Advance* from being carried up the face of the berg and tumbled over on her side. "But one of these mysterious relaxations, which I have elsewhere called the pulses of the ice, lowered us quite gradually down into the rubbish, and we were forced out of the line of pressure toward the shore. We grounded as the tide fell; and would have heeled over to seaward, but for a mass of detached land-ice that grounded alongside of us, and, although it stove our bulwarks as we rolled over it, shored us up." Kane could hardly get to his bunk when he went into the littered cabin after this hard-working vigil of thirty-six hours. Bags of clothing, food, tents, India-rubber blankets, and precious little personal effects were scattered around, placed where the owners could grab them in a hurry. Everything of real importance had been made ready for a march, hours before.

Throughout the hurricane the men behaved with the composure of experienced ice men. One man, to avoid being crushed, leaped onto a floating mass of ice, while four others were carried away by the drift; Kane lacon-

ically added that "they could only be recovered by a relief party after the gale had subsided!"

Taking advantage of the flood tide to approach the ice
beach, they harnessed themselves like mules on a canal
and tracked along the deep indentation in which they
found themselves. It was hard work; sometimes they made
three miles before the receding tide beached the brig.
They were at 78° 41': "We are farther north, therefore,
than any of our predecessors, except Parry on his Spitz-
bergen foot-tramp." An advance party, examining a harbor along the inner slope of their bay, found recent traces
of deer and the skull of a musk ox. Until then, musk oxen
were not known to be in Greenland; but their presence
there did not surprise Kane. "The migratory passages
of the reindeer, who is even less Arctic in his range than
the musk ox, led me to expect it."

Kane had hoped to reach a higher northing before being caught by winter. When, during the night of August
23, the thermometer fell to twenty-five degrees and
young ice formed without intermission, he "was somewhat loth to recognize these signs of the advancing cold."
In addition, he was uneasy that the ice might not permit
an escape from that bay next year. But the men, not
party to his hopes or fears, were asked to follow a strange
unrelenting schedule of work and rest: when the tide
freed the brig, they worked like horses; when the ship
was grounded, they rested. A few days of this and Kane
was forced to notice that "the depressing influences of
want of rest, the rapid advance of winter, and, above all,

our slow progress, make them sympathize little with this continued effort to force a way to the north."

Finally, "an excellent member" of the crew said they should turn south and give up thoughts of wintering. Here was a test of Kane's attitudes toward authority and a shared discipline. "I called them together at once, in a formal council, and listened to their views in full." All, but one, wanted to turn back. Kane could not agree. "I explained to them the importance of securing a position which might expedite our sledge journeys in the future, and after assuring them that such a position could only be attained by continuing our efforts, announced my intention of warping toward the northern headland of the bay." From that vantage point he could determine the best point for setting out on the spring operations; he gave them his word: "At the nearest possible shelter to that point I will put the brig into winter harbor." The explanation and promise satisfied the men; they "entered zealously upon the hard and cheerless duty it involved."

Kane decided to reconnoiter. The *Forlorn Hope,* their lightest whaleboat, was fitted with a canvas cover and stocked with pemmican; a small sledge was stowed away under her thwarts. Each man carried extra socks around his waist, to dry them by the heat of his body; each had a tin cup and sheath-knife at his belt. Buffalo robes made their sleeping gear, and a soup-pot and lamp completed their outfit. While they were gone the brig was to advance as before.

Their boat was useless after the first twenty-four hours.

Five days spent strenuously dragging their sledge netted them but forty miles. Progress along a difficult, treacherous terrain was slow, and they lost additional time following the winding coast. Kane decided to cache their sledge. Carrying only their pemmican and one buffalo robe, they made twenty-four miles.

At last Kane reached a headland from which he made his final reconnaissance. A hard day's walk carried him up to a height of 1100 feet. Before him was an unforgettable sight. Far off, the western shore of the sound lost itself in distance toward the north. From his vantage point "a rolling primary country led to a low, dusky wall-like ridge, which I afterwards recognized as the Great Glacier of Humboldt; and still beyond this was the land which now bears the name of Washington. The great area between was a solid sea of ice." Close along its shore he could see the long lines of hummocks dividing the floes like the trenches of a beleaguered city. "Farther out, a stream of icebergs, increasing in numbers as they receded, showed an almost impenetrable barrier. Nevertheless, beyond these again, the ice seemed less obstructed." How hopeful he was of finding open water in that Far Northern latitude! "Slowly, and almost with a sigh, I laid down the telescope and made up my mind for a winter search." Winter was the season for sledging.

And so Kane was convinced that the ice-sealed waters made further progress impossible; he had satisfied himself that the *Advance* would not find a better harbor along that mountainous coast. No place combined as many requisites for a good wintering. Rensselaer Bay, as he called it, seemed made for the *Advance.*

To the crew, anxiously waiting, he gave his report and decision. It was September 10. Immediately the brig was towed to a deep spot where it was perfectly sheltered from the outside ice. Everything seemed auspicious for the *Advance*'s wintering in Rensselaer Harbor. Yet later Kane sadly wrote: "We were fated never to leave together — a long resting-place to her indeed, for the same ice is around her still."

Winter approached rapidly. The young ice cemented the floes so the men could walk and sledge around the brig. In another month the sun would disappear, the long night descend. Their first action, small but of symbolic significance, was to change from "sea-time" to the familiar home series that begins at midnight; "there is something in the return of varying night and day that makes it grateful to reinstate this domestic observance."

Kane moved instantly to get the main projects started. Their future work and well-being depended on utilizing the fast-fading daylight. The rocky outcroppings that rose above tides and hummocks and icebergs served their needs admirably. On one they built a strong warehouse, and alongside, a comfortable doghouse.

On another islet, called "Fern Rock" after Kane's home, most of their scientific equipment was installed. One building, made of granite blocks cemented with moss and water "and the never-failing aid of frost," housed the transit and theodolite; nearby was the magnetic observatory, its copper fire-grate giving an "affectation of comfort"; here were the magnetometer and dip instruments. The meteorological observatory was set up on the open ice-field, a little distance from the ship. A wooden structure pierced with holes on all sides, it permitted a free passage of air while, within, a series of screens kept out the "fine and almost impalpable drift." The thermometers were suspended inside the screens and, by a cunning arrangement of a pane of glass, a lens, and an eyeglass, could be read from the outside. Care was necessary, for "their sensibility was such that . . . the mere approach of the observer caused a perceptible rise of the column." The tide register, a simple pulley gauge arranged with wheel and index, was on the brig. Only the wind gauge, clogged by condensing moisture, became ineffective.

While this building was in progress, Kane began treating some of their provisions according to experiments he had tried at home. Knowing that salt meat "in circumstances like ours is never safe," he had steaks of salt junk strung on lines like a countrywoman's dried apples, and soaked in festoons under the ice "where the water was fresh. The salmon trout and salt codfish purchased at Greenland, and their supply of pickled cabbage, were placed in barrels "perforated to permit a constant circulation of fresh water." These foods were "submitted to twelve hours of alternate soaking and freezing, the crust of ice being removed from them before each immersion." Kane was correct in fearing a diet of salted food, but his method, while it eliminated the salt, could not restore the lost vitamins. The science of nutrition was far in the future.

The third major project of their pre-winter activity was the establishment of provision depots northward along the Greenland coast. Kane planned three depots, spaced to reach as far north as possible; they were to be stocked with twelve hundred pounds of provisions, two-thirds pemmican. Future exploration depended on the success of these fall operations. Given a chain of depots, Kane could extend the distance he hoped to cover with dog-drawn sledges. As draft animals, dogs had only one disadvantage — they were limited in carrying the meat essential for their support. But with depots to renew the provisions, Kane could keep his teams fresh until the final station.

This method, perfected and elaborated, would carry Peary to the North Pole.

The first depot party was to start as soon as the young ice, forming a wide belt close to the shore, provided a practical road. Man-drawn, the sledge could carry fourteen hundred pounds of mixed stores. The personal equipment seemed stark, essential, and efficient: a rubber ground-cloth, a buffalo robe for the party to lie on, a heavy woolen sleeping bag for each man, and a canvas tent. Item by item it would be made still simpler. "As long as our Arctic service continued, we went on reducing our sledging outfit, until at last we came to the Esquimaux ultimum of simplicity — raw meat and a fur bag."

Before the young ice was right for the journey, Kane
sent out two men with Hans, the Eskimo, to make a quick
survey of the interior. Ninety miles inland they reached
the Icecap, the name given to the massive icy shroud that
covers Greenland save for a narrow, coastal fringe. It
reared up, four hundred feet high, and extended to the
north and west as far as they could see. They were back
before the seven-man depot party left the brig. "Our crew
proper is now reduced to three men; but all officers, the
doctor among the rest, are hard at work upon the observatory and its arrangements."

They had been terribly annoyed by rats. "Some days
ago we made a brave effort to smoke them out with the
vilest imaginable compound of vapors — brimstone, burnt
leather, and arsenic. But they survived the fumigation."
A second attempt with carbonic acid gas produced
"twenty-eight well-fed rats of all varieties of age." When
the hatches were opened to let the fumigating gas escape,
flames burst out; somehow a barrel of charcoal, ten feet
from the stoves and protected by a bulkhead, had ignited.
Buckets of water soon put out a blaze that could have destroyed their brig.

Daily Kane tried to master the difficult art of driving
an Eskimo dog team; it demanded proficiency with a six-
yard-long Eskimo whip. "You must not only be able to
hit any particular dog out of a team of twelve, but to
accompany the feat with a resounding crack. After this,
you find that to get your lash back involves another difficulty; for it is apt to entangle itself among the dogs and

lines." He finally learned the secret — but the mere labor of using the whip was exhausting.

By October 10, the depot party had been out twenty days. Kane was worried, and set out in search. Five days out, he met the returning men. They were in good condition, although not a man had escaped frostbite. One had frostbitten fingers received when a fox, so frozen as to defy skinning, was plucked by hand. Having cached every ounce they could spare, they were short on food and fuel; the hot food, coffee, and marled-beef soup Kane provided was welcome.

Kane pieced their story together. Five days after leaving the brig, they reached the headland Kane had attained when reconnoitering. At its base, as planned, they left their first cache. Three days later, after crossing a large bay, they made their second. Fifteen days out they came to a great glacier. For five days they tried to pass it, hoping to get farther north for the last depot. "This journey was along the base of an icy wall which constantly threw off its discharging bergs, breaking up the ice for miles around and compelling the party to ferry themselves and their sledge over the cracks by rafts of ice." Day and night the mighty calving of the glacier filled the air with salvos of grand artillery. Finally, they had to be content with a cache on a low island at the glacier's base.

Back at the ship, "a pack of cards, grog at dinner, and the promise of a three days' holiday, have made the decks happy with idleness and laughter."

I X

The Etah Eskimos Appear

KANE HAD a certain grim satisfaction that, except for Spitsbergen, "which has the advantages of an insular climate and is tempered by ocean currents, no Christians have wintered in so high a latitude as this." Yet the men of the *Advance*, by a skillful arrangement of fires and ventilation fixtures, enjoyed a comfortable temperature below deck even when it registered 25° below zero outside and a stiff wind was blowing.

"Our darkness has ninety days to run before we shall get back again even to the contested twilight of to-day. Altogether our winter shall have been sunless for one hundred and forty days." Darkness made its power felt on the spirit; it required a deliberate effort to keep a cheery tone among the men. It made the Eskimo Hans homesick. "Three days ago he bundled up his clothes and took his rifle to bid us all goodbye. It turns out that besides his mother there is another one of the softer sex that the boy's heart is dreaming of. He looked as wretched as any lover

of a milder climate." Kane treated Hans's nostalgia successfully — "by giving him first a dose of salts, and, secondly,
promotion. He has now all the dignity of henchman." Hans
stayed on. He harnessed the dogs, built traps, accompanied Kane on his ice tramps, and, except for hunting, was
excused from all other duty. "He is as happy as a fat
man ought to be."

Cold and darkness made the routine of scientific observations a test of a man's devotion to the pursuit
of knowledge. For the fireside astronomers who would
examine the data, Kane noted some of the hardships
the worker faced when the temperatures were extremely
low.

"The mere burning of the hands is obviated by covering the metal with chamois-skin; but the breath, and even
the warmth of the face and body, cloud the sextant-arc
and glasses with a fine hoar-frost. It is, moreover, an unusual feat to measure a base-line in the snow at fifty-five
below freezing." He explained why they failed to keep
their program of magnetic observations with strict regularity. The observatory was "an ice-house of the coldest
imaginable description. The absence of snow prevented
our backing the walls with that important non-conductor.
Fires, buffalo-robes, and an arras of investing sail-cloth
were unavailing to bring up the mean temperature to the
freezing point at the level of the magnetometer, and it
was quite common to find the platform on which the observer stood fully fifty degrees lower ($-20°$). Some of our
instruments, the dip-circle particularly, became difficult

to manage in consequence of the unequal contraction of the brass and steel."

Term-day tested their scientific zeal to the utmost. The observer, dressed in sealskin pants, dogskin hat, reindeer jumper, and walrus boots sat on a box, while a stove, "glowing with at least a bucketful of anthracite, represents pictorially a heating apparatus, and reduces the thermometer as near as may be to ten degrees below zero. One hand holds a chronometer, and is left bare to warm it; the other luxuriates in a fox-mitten.

"Perched on a pedestal of frozen gravel is a magnetometer; stretching out from it, a telescope: and bending down to this, an abject human eye. Every six minutes said eye takes cognizance of a finely-divided arc, and notes the result in a cold memorandum-book. This process continues for twenty-four hours, two sets of eyes taking it by turns; and, when twenty-four hours are over, term-day is over too." And term-day came every week!

Life aboard the brig differed from the winter routine of the previous expedition: this time they were busily getting ready for expeditions in the field. Even as they prepared for the spring journeys, their plans had to be drastically revised.

The dogs, on whom Kane counted for the northward dash, though "kept below, tended, fed, cleansed, and *doctored*, to the infinite discomfort of all hands," suddenly sickened. As January ended, Kane gave up "the last hope of saving them. Their disease is as clearly mental as in the case of any human being. The original epilepsy, which was the first manifestation of brain disease among them, has been followed by true lunacy. They bark frenziedly at nothing, and walk in straight and curved lines with anxious and unwearying perseverance. Generally, they perish with symptoms resembling locked-jaw in less than thirty-six hours after the first attack."

Of the dogs he had worked so hard to assemble, nine splendid Newfoundlands and thirty-five Eskimo dogs perished; only six survived. These still formed his principal reliance, and daily Kane worked to train them to run together as a team.

Supply problems began to harass Kane. Coal was rationed and the cabin could rarely be made warmer than 46°. Their supply of oil was exhausted, and because the lamps could "not be persuaded to burn salt lard," the men worked by light furnished by "muddy tapers of cork and cotton floated in saucers." Most serious of all their problems was that not a pound of fresh meat and only a barrel of potatoes remained of their antiscorbutics.

There was also the unbelievable state of the ice belt. In that Far Northern region, the ice belt was perpetual, clinging to the bold face of the cliffs, shrinking somewhat during the summer but always present. They thought of it as their highway of travel: a secure, and comparatively level, sledge road perched high above the grinding ice of the sea, and adapting itself to the tortuosities of the land. Since their arrival in Rensselaer Harbor, they observed how the ice belt grew; by the middle of March it circled the bay, thirty feet high and one hundred and twenty feet wide. But as a highway, it was as impassable as the great pack itself; it too showed mammoth scars of shock and collision.

And then there was the cold, cold greater than Kane had ever known.

On March 19 the first of the spring sledging parties took off. A fortnight later, as Kane was checking his gear to follow swiftly along their trail, three of the men staggered into the brig. Swollen, haggard, they could hardly speak. They muttered that the other four were "lying frozen and disabled. Where? They could not tell: somewhere in among the hummocks to the north and east; it was drifting heavily around them when they parted." Sinking with fatigue and hunger, they were rallied enough to indicate the direction from which they had come.

Instantly, Kane organized a rescue party. Strapping one of the three messengers, warmly dressed, onto their sledge in the hope he could serve as guide, they started. Utterly exhausted, the guide instantly fell asleep. On awaking, he was delirious. For eighteen hours the searchers trudged on, not stopping for food, unable to melt water. Then, miraculously, Hans caught sight of a broad sledge-track; this led to footsteps, and, following them "with religious care," they came to a flag fluttering from a hummock. "It was the camp of our disabled comrades; we reached it after an unbroken march of twenty-one hours."

They were now fifteen souls; the thermometer 75° below

the freezing point; and their only shelter was a tent barely able to contain eight. Half the rescuers slept, while the others walked around to keep from freezing; each man had a two-hour nap before facing the homeward march. They took only the tent and furs for protection, and food for fifty hours; the rest was abandoned. Out of the buffalo robes they made sacks — into which the sick, "their limbs sewed up carefully in reindeer skins," were placed on the sledge in a half-reclining position; other skins and bags were thrown over them, and the whole litter lashed together. Thus loaded the sledge weighed 1100 pounds. Before them lay a chaotic mass of hummocks.

For six hours they managed to pull well. Still nine miles away from their halfway mark — where the rescue team had cached their tent and pemmican so as to travel more quickly — suddenly, without premonition, all felt the unendurable effects of continued lack of sleep. Two of the rescuers begged permission to lie down; "they were not cold: the wind did not enter them now: a little sleep was all they wanted." A moment later Hans was found, nearly stiff under a drift; another man stood bolt upright, eyes closed, unable to articulate. Their bodies cried out for rest . . . rest. Half-asleep, they pitched the tent and crowded in. And so, with repeated minute doses of sleep and brandy, they hauled the heavy sledge for ninety miles. Their nightmare lasted seventy-two hours in all — their halts accounted for a brief eight hours, half the men sleeping at a time.

Sleep and food soon restored the rescuers. Of the rescued, two immediately suffered amputation; two men, Baker and Schubert, after lingering, died. Almost at that terrible moment of the expedition's first death, the deck watch hurried down into the cabin: *"People hallooing ashore!"*

Eskimos. Their existence along that northern coast, Kane had assumed; everywhere their abandoned encampments had told of their close presence, but searchers had been unsuccessful in finding those to whom this frigid country was home. And now finally, with no warning, when the party was stricken, the Eskimos appeared.

Followed by all who could mount the gangway, and accompanied by Petersen, the Danish Greenlander interpreter, Kane went above. "There they were, on all sides of our rocky harbor, dotting the snow-shores and emerging from the blackness of the cliffs — wild and uncouth, but evidently, human beings."

Their entrance was superbly timed for drama; the meeting revealed unexpectedly fantastic values. Here, in northern Greenland, civilization — in the person of Kane, a fine representative of his society — confronted the Stone Age. Kane faced a man nearly a head taller than himself, "extremely powerful, well-built, with swarthy complexion and piercing black eyes." The Eskimo hunter, who fearlessly advanced toward Kane, single-handed could have hunted the mighty walrus and white bear; later, he confided he thought Kane's party a "very pale-faced crew."

The white men had guns, wood, coal; not one of these

the Eskimos had or had ever seen. But Kane was mindful of how his bullets had ricocheted from the walrus's tough hide, that his supply of coal was scant, and that the illuminating oil was gone. For weapons the Eskimo relied on a lance and knife, his steel cutting edges were obtained from meteorites, or by trade from the south; weapons admirably designed to secure the great marine animals from a distance, or to kill a bear in close combat. The coal frankly amazed the natives. Since it was too hard for blubber, too soft for firestone, they were pleased it could at least heat as well as did the seal-fat they used — but for lighting purposes it was completely inadequate.

The white man had wood: a ship made of it — barrels and boxes — and additional assorted lumber, for a myriad of uses. The Eskimo had only bone and ivory. Yet out of these he filled his needs. The "sledges were made up of small fragments of porous bone, admirably knit together by thongs of hide; the runners, which glistened like burnished steel, were of highly-polished ivory, obtained from the tusks of the walrus." Narwhal horn or the thighbone of the bear, carved pieces laminated together, fitted and reinforced with sinew bindings, made the lance staff.

From his food supplies, the white man served his greatest treasure — good wheat bread, corned pork, and enormous lumps of sugar. None of these could prevent scurvy, and his fresh meat was gone. The Eskimos disdained the delicacies offered them; instead, they borrowed an iron pot and melted water, "and parboiled a couple of pieces of walrus meat; but the real *pièce de resistance*, some five pounds per head, they preferred to eat raw. Yet there was something of the *gourmet* in their mode of assorting their mouthfuls of beef and blubber. Slices of each, or rather strips, passed between the lips, either together or in strict alternation." Unregimented in the least act of their living, Kane noticed that "they did not all eat at once, but each man when and as often as the impulse prompted. Each slept after eating, his raw chunk beside him; and, as he woke, the first act was to eat, and the next to sleep again."

Whence had they come? Where were they going? How long had they been merrily traveling around? Kane envied them their fifty-six fine, healthy dogs picketed by their sledges. He contrasted the great price in life his party had paid to make a limited sledging journey, and the ease with which these nomads freely wandered in the same region at the same season. Uneasy, he ordered Baker's body hidden — "there were some signs of our disabled condition which it was important they should not see." The sight of a dead man might make them conscious of their advantage. Kane "tried to make them understand what a powerful Prospero they had had for a host, and how beneficent he would prove himself as long as they did his bidding." He bought all the walrus-meat they had to spare, and four of their dogs, "enriching them in return with needles and beads and a treasure of old cask-staves."

Kane had found the filth and noise of the South Greenland Eskimo distasteful; these Arctic Eskimos he found disagreeable. They were rude and difficult to manage.

Three or four would speak at a time, "to each other and to us, laughing heartily at our ignorance in not understanding them, and then talking away as before. They were incessantly in motion, going everywhere, trying doors, and squeezing themselves through dark passages, round casks and boxes, and out into the light again, anxious to touch and handle everything they saw, and asking for, or endeavoring to steal, everything they touched." For the first time in his travels, Kane acted like the gentleman from Philadelphia. "Our whole force was mustered and kept constantly on the alert."

The Eskimos, having chattered and looked, touched and pilfered, eaten and slept, were anxious, when morning came, to go. But first Kane obtained their promise "to return in a few days with more meat, and to allow me to use their dogs and sledges for my excursions to the north. They did not return: I had read enough of treaty making not to expect them too confidently."

With them went an ax, a saw, and some knives belonging to the expedition; soon it was found that the storehouses had been broken into; later, more alarmingly, a train of sledges was discovered concealed behind the hummocks. The next day the ship was visited by a party of five; two old men, one of middle age, and a couple of gawky boys. Apprehensive, Kane could yet not afford to break with the Eskimos, upon whose friendship depended a supply of fresh meat. He treated the party with kindness, and was shocked when the group took a coal barrel and slashed an India-rubber boat.

A few days later, "an agile, elfin youth" drove up to their ship in open day. He told them his name, *Myouk,* and where he lived; he denied having slashed the boat, and, when he refused to confess or repent, was taken, as a prisoner, to the hold. "At first he refused to eat, and sat down in the deepest grief; but after a while he began to sing, and then to talk and cry, and then to sing again till a late hour of the night. When I turned in, he was still noisily disconsolate." Myouk's song might well have been his summoning his Supernatural to help him escape from the pale demons, for in the morning he was gone.

"The month of April was about to close, and the short season available for Arctic search was upon us." Kane planned to reach the Great Glacier of Humboldt, restock from the cache laid down there, and examine the glacier to see if it might form an ice bridge connecting Greenland with the American continent. Committed to the idea of an open polar sea, he was eager to "determine the state of things beyond the ice-clogged area of this bay."

With one man, William Godfrey, he followed a day behind the advance party. His load, trimmed down to pemmican, bread and tea, included a soup kettle for melting water and making tea, and a tent. Each had his reindeer sleeping bag. Kane knew the journey would be arduous; its success depended on favorable circumstances and the stamina of "unbroken men." He did get to the Great Glacier of Humboldt before he broke down.

The day was beautifully clear when he saw the stupendous line of cliff that rose in a solid glassy wall "three hundred feet above the water-level, with an unknown, unfathomable depth below it; its curved face, sixty miles in length from Cape Agassiz to Cape Forbes, vanished into unknown space at not more than a single day's railroad-travel from the Pole. The interior with which it communicated, and from which it issued, was an unsurveyed ice-ocean. It was in full sight — the mighty crystal bridge which connects the two continents of America and Greenland."

Remembering how glaciologists compared glaciers and rivers, Kane slowly grasped that what he beheld was the counterpart "of the great river-systems of Arctic Asia and America. Yet here were no water feeders from the south. Every particle of moisture had its origin within the Polar circle, and had been converted into ice. There were no vast alluviums, no forest or animal traces borne down by liquid torrents. Here was a plastic, semi-solid mass, obliterating life, swallowing rocks and islands, and ploughing its way with irresistible march through the crust of an investing sea."

Kane's complete exhaustion was due to a combination of scurvy, snow blindness, and the unexpected presence of deep snow into which he sank at every labored step. His plan was doomed by the total destruction of the caches on which they had counted. Though every precaution had been taken, the quenchless curiosity of powerful predatory bears had mocked their efforts. At one place heavy rocks cemented in ice were tossed aside, iron casks filled with pemmican were smashed into chips as though with a cold chisel; while, of an alcohol cask, not even a stave remained. The bears had gastronomic preferences: alcohol, whether for fuel or drink, was a strong favorite; salt meats they spurned, ground coffee they relished, and of old canvas they could not get enough — not a shred was left.

Kane himself was the most seriously affected by scurvy. He collapsed. The others, scarcely able to travel, strapped him on the sledge and by forced marches brought him back to the *Advance*. It was late in May before he was well enough to leave his bunk. But even before he was up, he was planning how his shattered party could carry on their explorations.

It was unendurable that the northern coastline of Smith Sound remained a blank on the charts. Stopped by the Great Glacier, stopped by thieving bears, stopped by an assortment of infirmities, Kane acted on the military maxim that considered attack the only hope. He would send out "parties of exploration, one after another, as rapidly as the strength and refreshing of our teams would permit." Dogs were to be used entirely in future travel.

Dr. Hayes, sent with Godfrey to cross Smith Sound to Cape Sabine, returned eleven days later snow-blind and exhausted. But the position of Cape Sabine was determined, and the western shoreline followed a little to the south. Discarding every ounce of unessential equipment to save the diminished strength of their dogs, Hayes and Godfrey raced back across Smith Sound to Rensselaer Harbor. Kane heard their report; their misfor-

tunes and adventures were incidental to their success and
to the implications of their results: "There is still a hundred miles wanting to the northwest to complete our entire circuit of this frozen water." This unknown stretch
was the objective for the next party.

But how was Kane to organize it? On strictly medical
grounds he estimated the men's physical condition, picked
four who were "well," one who was "sound," and William
Morton who was "nearly recovered." Morton was ordered to expend only the minimum amount of strength on
the initial step and keep himself fresh for exploring the
northwest. When the dogs were rested and recovered,
Hans would follow and meet the advance party of five
at the Great Glacier — he and Morton to go on alone
with the dog sledge, and the sustaining party to turn
back. Kane had devised a form of relay, or shuttle, tech-
nique — the logistics of Arctic exploration — to create an
effective striking force.

It was June 3, the short sledging season was almost
spent; three days after Hayes and Godfrey returned, the
advance party started. Two weeks later Hans, driving the
recuperated dogs, was to follow.

On the twenty-seventh, the four men who accompanied
Morton returned, suffering from nothing worse than snow
blindness. Not until July 10, when out for a walk, did
Kane hear the distant sound of dogs. Hans and Morton
staggered in with the limping team.

On this final effort the Great Glacier of Humboldt was
passed. Morton and Hans found that the northern end of

Smith Sound opened into a noble, ice-free channel: Kennedy Channel. They traced it for fifty-two miles, as far as Cape Constitution. This rocky, sheer headland stopped them; there was no ice belt, and waves "broke directly against the cape." Morton climbed partway up the cliff and hoisted the Grinnell flag of the *Antarctic*.

From his vantage point, Morton saw the coastal mountains whose summits resembled "a succession of sugar-loaves and stacked cannon-balls declining slowly in the perspective." This western coast stretched far "towards the north, with an iceless horizon, and a heavy swell rolling in with white caps. At a height of about five hundred feet above the sea this great expanse still presented all the appearance of an open and iceless sea."

In presenting his conclusions, Kane was precise, correct, and cautious. But in the ice-free channel, the absence of an ice belt beyond Cape Constitution while it held unbroken further south, in the dark nimbus clouds and water sky, and crowds of birds found only where open water existed — in this complex of conditions was evidence sufficient to convince him personally that Morton and Hans had obtained proof of the existence of the open polar sea.

X

Docto Kayen:
The Philadelphian Eskimo

"IT IS A YEAR AGO TO-DAY since we left New York.
I am not as sanguine as I was then: time and experience
have chastened me." At that date Morton had not yet
won success for the party. "I am here in forced inaction,
a broken-down man, oppressed by cares, with many dangers before me, and still under the shadow of a hard
wearing winter, which has crushed two of my best associates."

It was natural that his thoughts should turn to Sir John
Franklin's party. To the tormenting question: could any
of the men have survived? he replied "no man can answer
with certainty; but no man without presumption can answer in the negative." His words were not a bland, elegant
evasion. Kane's supporting argument reveals his thinking.
Here is his first formulation of an approach to survival in
the Arctic. For Kane's importance is not, as his contemporaries saw it, the moving personal drama of a physically handicapped man engaged in activities demanding

strength and stamina; it is his brilliant intellectual victory over the habitual way of reacting to a problem.

If, four months ago — surrounded by darkness and bowed down by disease — I had been asked the question, I would have turned toward the black hills and the frozen sea, and responded in sympathy with them, NO. But with the return of light a savage people come down upon us, destitute of any but the rudest appliances of the chase, who were fattening on the most wholesome diet of the region, only forty miles from our anchorage, while I was denouncing its scarcity.

For Franklin, everything depends upon locality: but from what I can see of Arctic exploration thus far, it would be hard to find a circle of fifty miles' diameter entirely destitute of animal resources. The most solid winter-ice is open here and there in pools and patches worn by currents and tides, to these spots the seal, walrus, and the early birds crowd in numbers.

If his own party could be supported by the hunting of one man, Kane argued that a party of . . .

. . . tolerably skillful hunters might lay up an abundant stock for winter. As it is, we are making caches of meat in the very spot which a few days ago I described as a Sahara.

I have undergone one change of opinion. It is of the ability of Europeans or Americans to inure themselves to an ultra-Arctic climate.

Aware of the blighting effects of the long polar night, Kane perceived that "where cold and cold only is to be encountered, men may be acclimatized, for there is light enough for outdoor labor." He regarded the "North British sailors of the seal and whale fisheries as inferior to none in capacity to resist the Arctic climate," and thought it not unreasonable to expect that some of them may "have found a hunting-ground, and laid up from summer to summer enough of fuel and food and seal-skins to brave three or even four more winters in succession."

Having explained the reasons in favor of survival, he honestly presented his emotional bias.

"My mind never realizes the complete catastrophe, the destruction of all Franklin's crews. I think of them ever with hope. I sicken not to be able to reach them."

This long entry — question, conjecture, and confidence — Kane wrote in his journal on May 30, 1854; it needs to be set against facts and events and other dates. Just two months before (March 31), ten years after the expedition had sailed, the British Admiralty ordered the names of the officers and men of the *Erebus* and *Terror* removed from their books. Officially they were dead. Lady Franklin made her feelings for what she deemed "a heartless act" perfectly plain. She refused her widow's pension and, if her stepdaughter's word can be believed, "changed the deep mourning she had been wearing for years for bright colors of green & pink so soon as the Adm[iralt]y's notice was gazetted."

The following October, the Admiralty received news that Dr. John Rae, journeying for the Hudson's Bay Company, had obtained proof that disaster had come to the expedition. From a group of Eskimos Rae heard a tragic story: they had met a party of some forty white men who, by signs, indicated their boat had been crushed by ice and that they were traveling southward to hunt deer; later that year the Eskimos had found thirty dead near the mouth of the Great Fish River, lying where they fell as they walked. From these Eskimos Rae purchased some articles — without doubt they had belonged to the Franklin Expedition. The date when the men were still alive was the spring of 1850; they had survived for five years.

Here, alas, was the small group Kane had pictured alive after "three or even four winters." Spring had come — why had they not hunted the animals in the waters around them? Why did they think only in terms of deer as food? The tragedy is not that the men died, but that they died while Eskimos lived and traveled in that same region. Why did they spend their waning strength dragging a boat, when they could support themselves in a place where the Eskimos came for spring hunting, waiting until open water would permit them to sail? In the light of what Kane himself faced, it is not too much to say that, had he been in that party, they would not all have perished. Their fatal breakdown throws Kane's success in high relief; their debacle makes Kane's qualities unique.

The men of the *Erebus* and *Terror* shared Kane's naval background and orientation. In both they differed from Hearne and other fur traders who, like the frontiersmen, lived and traveled as natives with natives. Nothing in Kane's training prepared him to accept native life wholeheartedly. No one in his position before him had taken that simple but immense step — not even when it was a matter of survival.

The season for Arctic travel was ending when Morton and Hans brought glory to the expedition; but still the ice did not break up as it should. Kane faced a terrifying problem. Should he start south when it looked as though winter would catch the *Advance* before she was halfway through the pack? The alternative was not pleasant.

To examine the state of the icefield, or possibly get a message to a British squadron in Baffin Bay, or locate relief stores, Kane decided to reach southern waters in a whaleboat. Days of unremitting toil were necessary to pull the boat across twenty miles of heavy ice before launching her in open water. In the vicinity of Littleton Island where, the previous year, he had sailed through open water, ice now formed a continuous barrier. The report he brought back to those on the brig was dismal; the chance for their liberation was feeble.

Comparing the condition of the five men who had gone with him with that of those who remained at the ship, Kane noticed a surprising fact. His party carried only a hundred and fifty pounds of pork and had been away a month and yet they "had grown fat and strong on auks and eiders and scurvy-grass."

Originally they planned to free the ship before drift ice choked the leads close to shore. But Kane had seen how already the nearby coast was jammed with stupendous ice masses. Even though the prospect confronting them was hopeless they tried to move the brig. They warped; they blasted — the massive ice cracked; quickly, they warped — she was moved from her position inside the group of rocky islands. Then, at the outer floe, she stopped.

"I inspected the ice again today. Bad! bad! — I must look another winter in the face. I do not shrink from the thought; but while we have a chance ahead, it is my first duty to have all things in readiness to meet it." More than half of August was gone. Winter would soon be upon them. The choice confronting each man was to stay or to retreat to the south. This, Kane felt, was a question each man must answer for himself.

Calling the officers and men together, he frankly explained why he would stay. "I then told them that I should freely give my permission to such as were desirous of making the attempt. Having done this, I directed the roll to be called, and each man to answer for himself." Of the seventeen men, eight agreed with Kane. With the other group, he divided their "resources justly and liberally, and they left us on Monday, the 28th, with every appliance our narrow circumstances could furnish to speed and guard them. They carried with them a written assurance of a brother's welcome should they be driven back."

The party moved off with the elastic step of men confident of their purpose; they were soon out of sight. Those who remained realized what they faced. Reduced in number, reduced in strength and health, the cold and darkness of the impending winter, their poverty-stricken supplies, the dreary sense of increased isolation, they were "like men

driven to the wall, quickened, not depressed." Kane's first
resolution was to preserve their morale. Everything was to
continue as before: "The arrangement of hours, the distribution and details of duty, the religious exercises, the ceremonials of the table, the fires, the lights, the watch, even
the labors of the observatory and the notation of the tides
and the sky — nothing should be intermitted that had contributed to the day."

His next resolve was to insure their well-being. For this
he determined to practice the lessons learned from the Eskimos. "Their form of habitations and their peculiarities of
diet, without their unthrift and filth, were the safest and
best" under the circumstances.

He turned the brig into an igloo. Moss and turf was collected. "This is an excellent non-conductor; and when we
get the quarter-deck well padded with it we shall have a
nearly cold-proof covering. Down below we will enclose a
space some eighteen feet square, and pack it from floor to
ceiling with inner walls of the same material." He understood how the Eskimo hut retained its heat while allowing
for ventilation. "The entrance is to be from the hold, by a
low moss-lined tunnel, the *tossut* of the native huts, with as
many doors and curtains to close it up as our ingenuity
can devise. This is to be our apartment of all uses — not a
very large one; but we are only ten to stow away, and the
closer the warmer." He hoped, when they had enough
snow, to bank it around the brig. Insulating their living
quarters reduced the assaults of cold, however low, however prolonged.

A very few days after the expedition divided into two groups, "by a coincidence which convinced me how closely we had been under surveillance," three Eskimos appeared. Kane was apprehensive that they came to spy on the condition and resources of the white men. He offered them the hospitality of a tent below deck with a copper lamp, a cooking basin, and a liberal supply of slush for fuel. "I left them under guard when I went to bed at two in the morning, contentedly eating and cooking and eating again." In the morning, they not only eluded the guard and escaped, they took the lamp, boiler, cooking-pot, and Nannock, Kane's best dog. "If the rest of my team had not been worn down by over-travel, no doubt they would have taken them all."

Kane was embarrassed. Was this a hostile act? Previously, their pilfering had been "conducted with such superb simplicity, the detection followed by such honest explosions of laughter," that it seemed it must be proper behavior by their standards. Kane was puzzled, but knew he "must act vigorously, even at a venture." He sent his two best walkers to Anoatok, the nearest Eskimo hut, to overtake the thieves. Arriving there, they found young Myouk and the wives of two other Eskimos with "the buffalo robes already tailored into kapetahs on their backs." A thorough search revealed other missing articles.

"With the prompt ceremonial which outraged law delights in among officials of the police everywhere, the women were stripped and tied; and then laden with their stolen goods and as much walrus-meat from their own stores as would pay for their board, they were marched on the instant back to the brig. The thirty miles was a hard walk for them." Hardly twenty-four hours after the Eskimos left the brig with their booty their wives "were prisoners in the hold, with a dreadful white man for keeper, who never addressed to them a word that had not all the terrors of an unintelligible reproof."

Myouk was sent to summon Metek, the "head-man of Etah and others" to ransom the women. For five days they waited — the women crying, sighing, singing and eating all the time — before Metek and another arrived with "quite a sledge-load of knives, tin cups, and other stolen goods, refuse of wood and scraps of iron, the sinful prizes of many covetings." It was not guns that had impressed the Eskimos, but the vivid demonstration of human strength. "The fact that within ten hours after the loss of our buffalo skins we had marched to their hut, seized three of their culprits, and marched them back to the brig as prisoners — such a sixty-mile achievement as this they thoroughly understood."

Mutual respect made it possible to propose a treaty to the Eskimos. Remembering the lessons learned in the Chinese negotiations, Kane arranged the preliminary feasts and speeches. The terms were simple and beneficial to both.

On the part of the Eskimos: "We promise that we will not steal. We promise we will bring you fresh meat. We

promise we will sell or lend you dogs. We will keep you
company whenever you want us, and show you where to
find game."

On the part of the white men: "We promise that we will
not visit you with death or sorcery, nor do you any hurt or
mischief whatsoever. We will shoot for you on our hunts.
You shall be made welcome aboard ship. We will give you
presents of needles, pins, two kinds of knife, a hoop, three
bits of hard wood, some fat, an awl, and some sewing
thread; and we will trade with you of these and everything
else you want for walrus and seal-meat of the first quality."

For the closing formula to this document Kane wrote:
"We, the high contracting parties, pledge ourselves now
and forever, brothers and friends."

From its improbable beginning to its improbable conclusion, the treaty episode had the solemnity of a nursery
pact. It is artless and braggadocio, it is as bald as once-
upon-a-time, and as topsy-turvy as logic in a never-never
land. It proclaimed amity between two groups — ten men
in one, and about a hundred and forty men, women, and
children in the other. And yet, this agreement of September 6, 1854, established mutual security between men of
the United States and the people of Etah. It served not
only Kane's party but all who, for a variety of reasons, have gone there to the present day.

The understanding with the Eskimos established, "a
general community of interests" tested in incident after incident, the whites accepted the new regime with ease. "We
are absolute nomads, and our wild encounter with the ele-

ments seems to agree with us all. Our table-talk at supper was as merry as a marriage-bell. One party was just in from a seventy-four miles' trip with the dogs; another from a foot-journey of a hundred and sixty, with five nights on the floe." As nomads, the white men enjoyed hospitality at every hut. "Their wet boots were turned toward the fire, their woolen socks wrung out and placed on a heated stone, dry grass was padded round their feet, and the choicest bits of walrus-liver were put into the cooking-pot."

Every day of September was spent looking for game. They were in desperate need to secure fresh meat while there were still leads close to shore. After a particularly harrowing experience with fog on the ice floes, Kane and his Eskimo hunting companions took refuge in the abandoned stone hut at Anoatok. Safely inside, they discussed a "famous stew of walrus meat, none the less relished for an unbroken walk of forty-eight miles and twenty haltless hours." Kane shrewdly played on the Eskimo's respect for physical strength and at times, during the long walk, he half supported two Eskimo friends, a boastful gesture they recognized and admired. Nor did he show signs of being cold. He did not want the Eskimos to attribute the white man's rich store of appliances "to effeminacy or inferior power" which stood in need of aids to equal the hardihood of the Eskimos. He was Docto Kayen, an Eskimo.

October 4, Wednesday. I sent Hans and Hickey two days ago to the hunting-ice, to see if the natives had any luck with the walrus. They are back tonight with bad news—no meat, no Esquimaux.

Without Eskimo help, Kane feared the winter. Ten days later two other men, sent to locate the Eskimos, traveled as far as the lower Etah settlements before finding people. They brought back with them two hundred and seventy pounds of walrus meat and a couple of foxes. "This supply, with what we have remaining of our two bears, must last us until the return of daylight allows us to join the natives in their hunts."

Kane's willingness to experiment with foods of all kinds, no matter how alien or repugnant, had marked his earliest travels. Now, his habits and taste were subordinated to his belief in fresh meat. He began to include rat meat. The efforts to exterminate the pests had failed, and by the second winter they had become a serious nuisance. Kane cited many instances of their increase and boldness but added that he was "much their debtor. Through the long winter night, Hans used to beguile his lonely hours of watch by shooting them with the bow and arrow. The repugnance of my associates to share with me the table delicacies of such 'small deer' gave me the frequent advantage of fresh-meat soup, which contributed no doubt to my comparative immunity from scurvy."

As the sun left the sky altogether and the cold intensified, their fuel shortage became a serious problem. They faced the necessity of having to "burn largely into the brig." After consultation with the carpenter, Kane prepared to have some seven or eight tons of fuel cut away. The order in which the timbers could be used was determined. "Not a stick of wood comes below without my eyes following it through the scales to the woodstack. I weigh it to the very ounce." By planning and care he hoped to "get through this awful winter *and save the brig besides!"*

Rationing fuel, rationing their meager provisions, Kane was out daily, hunting for hares and tending the fox traps. The change and excitement kept him in good spirits. "The men are getting nervous and depressed, McGary paced the deck all last Sunday in a fit of homesickness, without eating a meal. I could not get along at all unless I combined the offices of physician and commander. You can not punish sick men."

By December it required "the most vigorous effort of a healthy man to tear from the oak ribs of our stout little boat a single day's firewood." Grated raw potato was again a medicine for scurvy. The few left were three years old, but worth "their weight in gold."

"Esquimaux sledges!" the deck watch called out. It was the morning of December 7. Strange Eskimos. They came on an errand of mercy, bringing two of the men who had left three months before, and announcing that the others were two hundred miles away "divided in their councils, their energies broken, and their provisions nearly gone." Kane's first thought was of rescue. But most of his own party were stricken; he could spare no one — he had to entrust the rescue of the remaining men to the Eskimos.

Kane was as good as his word: he received the rest of the escape party with a brother's welcome. Once again the expedition was together. With due allowance for the des-

perate nature of the gamble they took, the men who left
the brig lacked the will, the resourcefulness, the necessary
intelligence that made Kane master the art of living in the
Arctic. They were frightened, they were exhausted, they
succumbed to cold and frostbite; but they did not have
scurvy. Kane, without passing judgment, commented:
"The coffee and meat-biscuit soup, and the molasses and
the wheat bread, even the salt pork which our scurvy for-
bade us to touch — how they relished it all. For more than
two months they had lived on frozen seal and walrus
meat."

Differing personalities had divided the men into the two
groups: those who wanted to maintain their habits intact
in a radically changed environment, and those whose habits changed as change was demanded. Contrast the picture
of hardship one group felt at being deprived of their accustomed luxuries with the mouth-watering homage Kane
pays raw meat.

The liver of a walrus (*awuktanuk*) eaten with little slices
of fat — of a verity it is a delicious morsel. Fire would ruin
the curt, pithy expression of vitality which belongs to its un-
cooked juices. This pachyderm is the very best fuel a man can
swallow.

Kane's deliberate use of the word *fuel*, not food, explains
his thinking. His chemist's training taught him that com-
bustion and metabolism are different words for the same
process; he sought the fuel best suited to stoke the human
engine in that climate. Empirically Kane rated raw meat
and fresh meat as antiscorbutics! — "In large quantities it

[fresh food] dissipates the disease [scurvy]; in ordinary rations it prevents its occurrence; in small doses it checks it while sustaining the patient."

Fuel as fuel was also scrutinized by Kane. The Smith Sound Eskimos were not covered with a grimy soot, because they attended their lamps "with assiduous care, using the long radicles of a spongy moss for wick, and preparing the blubber for its office by breaking up the cells between their teeth." The Eskimos preferred walrus fat; but Kane substituted pork fat, boiled to lessen its salt, yet got satisfying heat from such burners.

Once, Kane had prided himself on the simplicity of his sledging requirements — "simple certainly as compared with those of the English parties"; now by his concentrated study of Eskimo techniques he made them simpler, more functional. He appreciated that a broken sledge could be as fatal as a broken leg, that the intense cold snapped iron nails or rivets like glass, and a rigidly fastened woodwork was unable to stand the fierce concussions of the drive. On the other hand, in the Eskimo sledge, everything was put together with lashings of seal-skin, and the whole fabric was the "skeleton framework of a sledge as flexible as a lady's work-basket, and weighing only forty pounds." The carpenter made a sledge like the Smith Sound *kommetik,* substituting wood and iron for bone and ivory. On the wooden frame he fastened a tightly stretched canvas which had an attached apron and cover. "Into this apron and cover you pack your cargo, the less of it the better; and then lace and lash the whole securely together."

Except for a fur sleeping bag and a spare pair of boots, everything was worn as clothing. Rightly clad, the Arctic traveler "is a lump of deformity waddling over the ice, unpicturesque, uncouth, and seemingly helpless"; but his clothing is admirably designed to insulate the heat-creating body from the cold. The fox-skin jumper, or *kapetah*, is a closed shirt fitted very "loosely to the person, but adapted to the head and neck by an almost air-tight hood, the *nessak*." The hood is deep enough "to embrace the face and forehead. Underneath the *kapetah* is a similar garment, but destitute of the hood, which is put on as we do an inner shirt." Made of bird-skins softened by being "chewed in the mouth of the women," it was "worn with this unequalled down next the body." More than five hundred auks went into a garment of this description.

The lower extremities were "guarded by a pair of bear-skin breeches, the *nannooke*," not rising above "the crests of the pelvis" and "thus leaving exposed those parts which in the civilized countries are shielded most carefully." The upper and lower garments were not joined nor belted together, a slight overlapping gave the wearer protection and complete freedom. Footgear consisted of a bird-skin short sock, with a padding of grass nicely distributed over the sole.

Outside of this comes a bear-skin leg, sewed with great skill to the natural sole of the plantigrade, and abundantly wadded about the foot with dry non-conducting straw. The only additional articles of dress are a fox's tail held between the teeth to protect the nose in a wind, and mitts of seal-skin well wadded with sledge-straw.

The one detail Kane found inadequate in such attire was the "uncovered space between the waistband of the *nannooke* and the *kapetah*. To bend forward exposes the back to partial nudity; and no matter what the attitude, the entire chest is open to the atmosphere from below." Yet Kane observed how one of the Eskimos who had brought back the stricken party stood in the open air — the temperature was minus 50° — "comfortably scratching his naked skin, ready for a second journey." He himself saw that in this well-ventilated costume the Eskimo "will sleep upon his sledge with the atmosphere 93° below our freezing point."

By April, Kane mastered the separate elements of Eskimo life; he could enter fully into their way of life; more than that, he enjoyed it. With his friend Metek he raced one day through a storm to a settlement of two huts. Into one they crawled; it had an extraordinary *tossut* thirty paces long. "I soon found myself gasping the ammoniacal steam of some fourteen vigorous, amply-fed, unwashed, unclothed fellow lodgers."

I had come somewhat exhausted by an eighty miles' journey through the atmosphere of the floes: the thermometer inside was at +90°, and the vault measured fifteen feet by six.

The kotluk [how casually and easily he now uses Eskimo words] of each matron was glowing with a flame sixteen inches long. A flipper-quarter of walrus, which lay frozen on the floor, was cut into steaks; and the kolupsuts [a hook suspended over the fire] began to smoke with a burden of ten to fifteen pounds apiece. I broke my fast on a handful of frozen liver-nuts and, bursting out into a profuse perspiration, I stripped like the rest, threw my well-tired carcass across Mrs. Eider-duck's extremities, put her left-hand baby under my armpit, pillowed my head on Myouk's somewhat warm stomach, and thus, an honored guest and in the place of honor, fell asleep.

Hunting, visiting, traveling with the Eskimos, Kane learned a great deal about this group who call a six-hundred mile strip of land, lying between the Inland Ice and the sea, their home.

They exist both in love and community of resources as a single family. The sites of their huts are arranged with reference to the length of the dog-march and the seat of the hunt; and thus when winter has built her highway, and cemented into one the sea, her islands, and the main, they interchange with each other the sympathies and social communion of man. The main line of travel is then as beaten as a road at home. The dogs speed from hut to hut, almost unguided by their drivers. They regulate their time by the stars. Every rock has its name, every hill its significance; and a cache of meat deposited anywhere in this harsh wilderness can be recovered by the youngest hunter in the nation.

As Kane accepted the Eskimos, so they accepted him. For himself he won the title and respect due an *angekok* — a mighty man, a powerful man, a man in command of stern sorcery. Did they not watch his hand "terrible with flaming ether, while it lifted nails with a magnet?" They also knew he used his strong magic to help, not harm. Mrs. Eider-duck, née Small Belly, had a sister whom Kane relieved of much suffering by opening a furuncle.

With the arrival of *upernak,* the Season of Thaws, as his friends called the end of May, Kane felt happily at home among the Eskimos of Smith Sound.

X I

The Retreat:

Living off the Land

To RETREAT from Rensselaer Harbor to South Greenland, Kane mobilized every resource at his command; his qualities of leadership and his professional skill, his experience gained on the boat journey, in hunting, and sledging, his knowledge of the land and the waters which stretched between them and the nearest settlement — Upernavik. Almost it was like a test in which the Arctic posed all her problems, a test to see if he had mastered the necessary lessons.

Kane had no choice but retreat:

I regard the abandonment of the brig as inevitable. We have by actual inspection but thirty-six days' provisions, and a careful survey shows that we cannot cut more firewood without rendering our craft unseaworthy. A third winter would force us, as the only means of escaping starvation, to resort to Esquimaux habits and give up all hope of remaining by the vessel and her resources. It would therefore in no manner advance the search after Sir John Franklin.

Soon after New Year's Day, 1855, Kane planned the escape. Refuge Harbor, hardly more than forty miles from the brig, had open water. To it they could transport their boats and supplies by sledge, and from there the boats would carry them. "Once at Cape Alexander, we can support our sick by our guns." Day after day, while darkness confined the men to the ship, they worked hard to be ready; even the very sick were given the task of picking over eider down.

The provisions for the trip were prepared and packed. Ship bread was hammered to a powder and compressed into the bags. Pork fat and tallow were melted, poured into other bags, and frozen; the same was done to a stock of concentrated bean soup. Flour and the remaining meat biscuits were wrapped in double bags to protect them from moisture. This was all they had to take with them. "For the rest we relied on our guns."

Constant exposure to ice and storm had made their three boats almost unseaworthy. Two twenty-six-foot whaleboats were strengthened, equipped with a mast apiece, and each was enclosed by a "neat housing of light canvas stretched upon a ridge-line," its sides fastened to a jack-stay. The third, if it proved unsafe for navigation, could serve as firewood. Each boat was provided with two large iron cylinders, a kind of windshield, into which fitted an iron saucer to hold pork-fat or blubber with a wick, and a large tin cannister to melt snow, and make tea or soup. The boats were mounted on sledges; the provisions were stored neatly under the thwarts. Each officer was assigned specific duties in the preparation and in the actual journeying.

Recognizing the importance of acting directly upon the men's minds, my first step was to issue a general order appointing a certain day, the 17th of May, for setting out. Every man had twenty-four hours given him to select and get ready his eight pounds of personal effects. After that his time was to cease to be his own for any purpose. It was necessary to brace up and concentrate every man's thoughts and energies upon the one great common object—our departure from the vessel on the 17th, not to return.

Kane recognized in the "waywardness" of his men an insidious symptom of scurvy. Had he not been a physician he might have disciplined the "moody indifference with which many went about their tasks," and the doubts, the suspicions, the whisperings, which fastened on every phase of his announced plan of retreat. Contending against a sullen attitude, Kane made sure that, when the time came to adjust the boats to their sledges, they would be empty and light, and the immediate ice smooth. He wanted a successful demonstration to silence "the croakers [who] protested that we could not stir an inch." Without having said a word, he noticed the men's morale improve as the sledges slid over the level stretch.

Such measures were necessary to prepare the men if they were to endure crossing the ice belt and force a road over the chaotic ridges that lay between them and open water. Nearly every man was an invalid, unused to open air and exertion; and Kane was careful not to overtax them lest exhaustion bring back their pessimism. The first day they pulled one boat two miles and came back to a hearty supper and warm beds. Kane "had the satisfaction of marching them back [from the ship] each recurring morning refreshed and cheerful. The weather, happily, was superb."

On May 20 the ship was formally abandoned.

It was Sunday. Our moss walls had been torn down, and the wood that supported them burned. Our beds were off at the boats. The galley was unfurnished and cold. Everything about the little den of refuge was desolate. We read prayers and a chapter of the Bible; and then all standing silently round, I took Sir John Franklin's portrait from its frame and cased it in an India-rubber scroll.

With these ceremonials the leavetaking commenced. As always in moments of high importance, Kane addressed the party: he outlined the difficulties ahead, but assured them they could be overcome with energy and "subordination to command," and that the 1300 miles of ice and water between them and rescue could be "traversed with safety for most, and hope for all."

His speech, his competent arrangements, his confidence tempered with caution, silenced their doubts and enlisted their courage.

After the speech they went on deck. The flags were hoisted and hauled down again, the men walked once or twice around the vessel, "looking at her timbers and exchanging comments upon the scars which reminded them of every stage of her dismantling." When they were quite ready, they "scrambled off over the ice together." For two years the *Advance* had been their home and refuge. Leaving her reinforced every fear for the future. The ceremony permitted the men to express the sadness and uncertainty such a farewell entailed; it eased them through a crisis and mobilized their efforts for the perilous adventure immediately ahead.

There were but twelve men to drag the boats: four of the party were bedridden; Kane, using his dog team, was to serve as carrier and courier; and, for the past month, Hans had not been part of the group. (Repeated inquiries received the same answer: "Hans the faithful — yet, I fear, the faithless — was last seen upon a native sledge, driving south with a maiden at his side, and professedly bound to a new principality high up Murchison Sound. Alas for Hans, the married man!") Since six men were not strong enough to pull one boat, all concentrated on one at a time; but for everything else — cooking, sleeping, baggage, and rations — they were divided into two messes. The routine established until they should reach water was precise and comprehensive.

During this early period, Kane insisted that proper rest was the first essential. The men never began a day's labor until they were refreshed from the efforts of the day before; the condition of the men regulated the halts, not arbitrary working hours; and sleep was meted out in proportion to the trials of the march. Though the thermometer stood at zero, "the housed boats, well crowded, and fully stocked with sleeping gear, were hardly uncomfortable to weary men; besides which, we slept by day when the sun was warmest and traveled when we could avoid the greatest glare."

The basic elements of Eskimo garb were used. Each man had a wool suit under the Eskimo fur clothes — fox-skin jacket and hood, and bearskin trousers; each had boots — a pair of canvas faced with walrus-hide over another inside "made of the cabin Brussels carpet." The only other essential articles were a comfortably adjusted harness for pulling the sledges and snow goggles made on the Eskimo pattern — a small slit cut transversely in a piece of wood.

Kane had used the weeks before leaving the ship to prepare Anoatok, a midway point to receive the sick. Perched on a rocky promontory, it commanded a view of the ice expanse of the straits, and on the level behind it grew flowers and coarse grasses, a certain sign that it had sunshine. The ice belt, now wonderfully smooth, made a road almost to this little plain. An abandoned, low stone hut, more like a cave than a formed habitation, was repaired, made weather-tight, and cleaned; a glass taken from a picture gave it a window. Kane softened the platform with wood-shavings, and over them spread his best cushions; he draped the walls with woolen blankets, installed a stove — Anoatok was ready for the invalids.

One at a time he brought them there on his dog sledge. Kane appreciated that it was impossible to leave the men at the ship — it would make them prey to the blackest gloom; nor could he permit them on the boat sledges — it would impede the party's progress and jeopardize their lives. Close to Anoatok Kane stacked most of the provisions so that the invalids could see they were not out of the line of march. Of the four, one was well enough to keep the lamps burning and heat up the food for the others.

With his dog sledge, Kane shuttled back and forth between the brig and the boats, stopping off at the little hospital to bring supplies and reassurance and give them word of the main group's progress. His six dogs, "well worn by previous travel, carried me with a fully burdened sledge between seven and eight hundred miles during the first fortnight after leaving the brig — a mean average of fifty-seven miles a day."

Even though it required extra work, Kane felt this was an essential part of the medical treatment. From his own experience he knew that illness "is best combatted by moral excitement." A few weeks later he was not surprised to see that everybody was stronger, more cheerful. "They had learned housekeeping, with its courtesies as well as comforts. Their kotluk would have done credit to Mrs. Eider-duck herself: they had a dish of tea for us, and a lump of walrus; and they bestirred themselves real housewife-fashion to give us a warm place and make us comfortable."

By June 12 the dragged boats reached Lifeboat Cove, where two years before they had cached food. The four invalids were brought up — for the first time since leaving the vessel the sick and well were together again; but their joy was brief. A man who had injured himself on the march died. "We gave two hours to the memory of our brother, and then resumed our toilsome march."

As the men approached the southern settlements of the Smith Sound Eskimo, their native friends flocked to help them. They pulled at the drag-ropes.

They carried our sick upon their hand-sledges. They relieved us of all care for our supplies of daily food. The quantity of little auks that they brought us was enormous. They fed us and our dogs at the rate of eight thousand birds a week, all of them caught in their little hand nets. All anxiety left us for a while. The men broke out in their old forecastle-songs; the sledges began to move merrily ahead, and laugh and jest drove out the old moody silence.

Neither gales nor treacherous ice nor a weakness due to short rations now prevented the party from carrying out the hardest part of its escape. Climbing a hill, Kane saw "open water, so long the goal of our struggles, spread" before him. Not far off rose the sheer height of Cape Alexander.

The Eskimos camped with them.

I can name them every one, and they know us as well. We have found brothers in a strange land. Myouk is crowding fresh presents of raw birds on me as if I could eat forever, and poor Mrs. Eider-duck is crying beside the tent-curtain, wiping her eyes on a birdskin!

There was sadness at the impending parting, but there was also an air of a happy carefree picnic.

We cook for them in our big camp-kettle; they sleep in the third boat; a berg close at hand supplies them with water; and thus rich in all that they value they seem supremely happy. But for them our dreary journey would have been prolonged at least a fortnight, and we are so late even now that hours may measure our lives.

Distributing presents was the only way Kane could thank them for their aid.

My amputating knives, the greatest gift of all, went to Metek and Nessark; but everyone had something as his special prize. Our dogs went to the community at large, as tenants in common, except Toodla-mik and Whitey. I could not part with them, the leaders of my team.

Kane noticed as they shuttled back and forth over the ice that though "numberless articles of inestimable value to them have been scattered upon the ice unwatched, they have not stolen a nail. It was only yesterday that Metek, upon my alluding to the manner in which property of all sorts was exposed without pilfering, explained the argument of their morality: 'You have done us good. We are not hungry: we will not take — You have done us good; we want to help you: we are friends.'"

It is fitting that the Eskimos should have the last word — with it they exit from Kane's life.

A high wind which detained them at the water's edge died away. "With the bay as smooth as a garden-lake," the little flotilla cast off. Threading their way through leads that shielded them from the heavy seas, pulling the boats along by ice hooks, sometimes dragging them over large floes, they pushed on to Northumberland Island. "Myriads of auks greeted us and we returned their greeting by the appropriate invitation to our table." They pushed on. Sometimes they made good progress, sometimes they found their course slow and wearisome. When they wanted to sleep, they pulled their boats onto ice floes.

Battered by a gale, they were unable to find a harbor. Everywhere the shore presented them with the high, forbidding wall of the ice-belt. Their newly gained strength was quickly drained off by the effort to keep afloat. At last they came to a place where, with the high tide, they could scale the ice cliff and lift their boats out of the water. A ravine, cutting sharply into the steep rock, offered an unexpected shelter and the familiar, unmistakable, gladdening sound of eider duck, as they turned in wet and hungry to their long-coveted sleep, gave them dreams of eggs and abundance. "We remained almost three days in our crystal retreat, gathering eggs at the rate of twelve hundred a day. Outside the storm raged without intermission and our egg hunters found it difficult to keep their feet; but a merrier set of gourmands than were gathered within never surfeited in genial diet." They called it "Weary Man's Rest."

Their apprehensions increased as they went on. Kane was startled to see how seriously the boats had suffered. One, quite unseaworthy, required nearly all their wood to keep her in repair. The men, having counted on securing a continuous store of birds, were worried by the lack of them; but the storm seemed to have driven the flocks

away. Conditions grew serious as they came close to Cape
Dudley Digges. An uncharted glacier, jutting still farther
out to sea than one they had just passed with much labor,
presented a formidable hurdle: the crews were too weak
to track through the heavy snow covering the land ice and
the boats too frail even for the sludge that filled the lead.
Kane climbed a berg to see what lay ahead. "My eyes
never looked on a spectacle more painful. We were in
advance of the season; the floes had not broken up." He
realized they were caught between two barriers, "both impassable to men in our condition." But with miserably
inadequate stores, how could they wait until the tardy
summer opened a way to them?

He headed for the cliffs. "Desolate and frowning as they
were, it was better to reach them and halt upon the un-
hospitable shore than attempt the fruitless ventures of the
sea." They drew the boats up on the fragment of the ice-
belt — a mere five-foot-wide shelf. Above, cliff seemed to
pile on cliff, rising more than a thousand feet, their summits lost in fog and mist — and all the way up were birds'
nests. "To soften the scene, a little natural bridge opened
on our right hand into a little valley cove, green with
mosses, and beyond and above it, cold and white, the glacier." There behind the grim, forbidding line of rock was
a little sheltered meadow, gay with flowers, lively with the
sound of running water, "the thermometer was at 90° in
the sun; in the shade at 38°."

The scene abounded in life: "the lumme, nearly as
large as canvas-backs, and, as we thought, altogether

sweeter and more juicy; their eggs well-known as delicacies on the Labrador coast; the cochlearia, growing superbly on the guano-coated surface — imagine such a combination of charms for scurvy-broken, hunger-stricken
men." The week spent at Providence Cliffs was like a glori-
ous vacation, and Kane, not wishing to break the carnival
mood, did not mention that he had looked out on a bleak
ice field ahead.

The story of the next weeks is the rapid, violent alternation of feast and famine, good fortune, bad fortune, and,
most wonderfully, good again. Hugging the cliffs until
they reached Cape York, they enjoyed quantities of birds
and generous fires of turf blazing merrily after a hard
day's work. Before them lay Melville Bay. There the land
leads ended and the "fast," as the whalers call the immov-
able shore-ice, swept unbroken as far as they could see.
No nesting birds made it worth while to stay close to shore
pulling the boats over the ice. They were forced to try for
open water far from land. The boats were hauled up, examined carefully, and repaired as best they could.

When they embarked their trials began.

In the open bay, in boats so frail, so unseaworthy that
constant bailing alone kept them afloat, they were at the
mercy of the great ice drift. Away from fresh food, scurvy
immediately affected them. Again their breathing became
labored and their feet so swollen they had to cut their canvas boots. Worst of all, they could not sleep. "It was in

this crisis of our fortunes that we saw a large seal floating on a small patch of ice, and seemingly asleep."

Trembling with anxiety, they prepared to crawl down on him. Stockings were drawn over the oars to muffle them. Petersen, with the large English rifle, was stationed in the bow. The excitement was intense; the men could hardly keep stroke. When about three hundred yards off, the oars were taken in. In deep silence they moved slowly forward; slowly, as a single scull astern gave the only motion.

The seal was not asleep.

He reared his head when we were almost within rifle-shot; and to this day I can remember the hard, careworn, almost despairing expression of the men's thin faces as they saw him move: their lives depended on his capture.

I depressed my hand nervously, as a signal for Petersen to fire. The poor fellow was paralyzed by his anxiety, trying vainly to obtain a rest for his gun against the cut-water of the boat. The seal rose on his fore-flippers, gazed at us for an instant with frightened curiosity, and coiled himself for the plunge. At that instant, simultaneously with the crack of our rifle, he relaxed his long length on the ice, and, at the very brink of the water, his head fell helplessly to one side.

No discipline could have controlled the men. With a wild yell they urged both boats upon the floes, and dragged the seal up to safer ice.

The men seemed half-crazy: I had not realized how much we were reduced to absolute famine. They ran over the floe, crying and laughing and brandishing their knives. Not an ounce of this seal was lost.

That was the last round in their desperate bout with hunger. By August 1 they had felt their way through the ice and fog of Melville Bay to its southern end. Before them rose a landmark, the Devil's Thumb.

And now, with the apparent certainty of reaching our homes, came that nervous apprehension which follows upon a hope long deferred. I could not trust myself to take the outside passage, but timidly sought the quiet-water channels running deep into the archipelago which forms a sort of labyrinth along the coast.

It was two days later.

"Halloo."

"Listen, Petersen! *Oars. Men.* What is it?"

Petersen listened. Quietly at first, and then trembling, he half-whispered: *"Dannemarkers."*

Eighty-four days had passed since they had left the *Advance*.

Slowly, aboard the Danish supply ship, they sailed along the Greenland coast to Godhavn. There they heard that Captain Hartstene had been sent to find them. And so, when some days after a lookout man on a hilltop announced a steamer in the distance, Kane and his men impatiently jumped into a boat and rowed out to meet her. Presently they were alongside.

"Captain Hartstene!" A little man in a ragged flannel shirt hailed the steamer.

"Is that Doctor Kane?"

"Yes."

Kane, looking up, saw the rigging alive with his countrymen. He heard their cheers, cheers that "welcomed us back to the social world of love which they represented."

Entering Sandy Hook, Bark Release, October 11, 1855. We are back again safe and sound, after an open-air travel by boats and sledges of thirteen hundred miles.

Kane wrote before landing so that John P. Kennedy would have immediate word directly from him.

Succinctly, he was stating the facts of their escape. Was he, as he wrote those words, thinking of the news told him in Greenland — that "Franklin's party, or traces of the dead which represented it, had been found nearly a thousand miles to the south of where we had been searching for them?"

Kane grieved that one sixth of his little party had perished in the two and a half years they had been absent. But he found satisfaction in that the rest had delivered themselves by their own exertions; he had pride that their collections of scientific data and Arctic plants and animals had been saved even though "every ounce of weight and inch of room was to the exclusion of so much food." This, he knew well, expressed the understanding and self-denial of his comrades; without their co-operation he could never have undertaken their transportation.

Of himself, he could say: "My health is almost absurd. I have grown like a walrus."

The rest of Kane's story is soon told. Immediately upon his return he started the account of his expedition. He wrote nine hundred pages and made three hundred sketches for the engraver; everything was finished by July 4. He decided to make the book readable, even if such treatment would "destroy its permanence and injure" him. "My wish is to make it a centre-table book, fit as well for the eyes of children as of refined women." *Arctic Explorations* found its way to that honorable place — its first three years' sales were over 145,000 copies. It was written with a pen dipped in the author's heart's blood.

To his publisher, Kane poured out complaints about the "wretched book," the "poor book," but kept at his task even though other activities made heavy demands on his strength and time.

"Something is the matter," he wrote in July, "for I get weaker every day." By August he could hardly move, and was requesting his publisher to come to him. At the end of September, *Arctic Explorations* was published. He was no longer able to work.

The unanswered letters which crowd around me might well appall an abler man. I leave in a fortnight, probably for Europe, as a sort of last resort, to catch my lost blessing. The book, poor as it is, has been my coffin.

When he wrote those despairing words, did Kane, as physician and patient, know that his damaged heart could no longer sustain his hopes and plans? If so, the knowledge was recent, for in June, a few months before, he was assuring his publisher that he had "accumulated enough of nerve-force to carry me through that ominously pleasant word 'Finis' "; nor had he hesitated to accept Lady Jane Franklin's proposal to lead the party she would send to verify the sad news Dr. Rae had heard. And Kane, who always referred to his illness as "my enemy," diagnosed the new attack that overpowered him as a "combination of rheumatism and the Arctic scourge of scurvy."

Then what was the "blessing"? Where had he lost it; how did he hope to catch it? Perhaps it pointed to the North — to which he would hope to return on Lady Jane's mission — to the Arctic where but lately he had been well, happy, and amazingly effective. Nowhere else had he been singled out as a tower of health; yet during that second winter, he alone had been well.

In June, when he was conscious of an untapped nerve-force and planning for the future, he was still at work on his book and, remembering and reliving the events he was recording, he was still emotionally in the Arctic. Writing the book postponed his return for Kane. That, delayed but inevitable, came on July 4, when he wrote "Finis." Was the sudden, mortal weakness he felt the sign of a failing heart, or was it a way Kane expressed bewilderment, his difficulty in readjusting to a normal existence? How does the explorer who has adapted himself to life on the distant horizon find the world he had left? If it is hard to face the wilderness, it is infinitely harder to shuttle between the wilderness and civilization.

Kane had traveled far from his Philadelphia background. Sketching the world of his Etah friends, his words are colored with affection and their tone is frankly nostalgic.

To Grinnell he was quite explicit about his attitude:

"We regarded the coarse life of these people with eyes of envy, and did not doubt that we could have lived in comfort upon their resources. It required all my powers, moral and physical, to prevent my men from deserting to the walrus-settlements; and it was my fixed intention to have taken to Esquimaux life, had Providence not carried us through in our hazardous escape."

Kane himself could measure how far he had deviated from his family's respectable values. He retracted his earlier condemnation of what he had called the Eskimos' "unthrift," and endorsed their behavior which was based on the view that "the day provides for itself; or, if it does not, we trust in the morrow, and are happy till tomorrow disappoints us." It is not surprising that he found their philosophy congenial — his own precarious health had long ago forced him to accept it.

On October 10, accompanied by "Morton, my faithful adjutant," Kane sailed for Liverpool. His family, habituated to a series of desperate illnesses and astounding recoveries, supported his desire to travel in Europe; they thought it would be a dose of that medicine which never before had failed him — the tonic of new friends, a new milieu, a new activity, and a consuming interest.

Lady Jane Franklin was waiting to care for him when he arrived in London. Older than his mother, she wanted nothing better than to ply the dying man with cod-liver oil and soothing books, while they discussed the expedition he would lead. And when he failed to improve and the doctors advised a warmer climate, Lady Jane could hardly be restrained from sailing with him. He gave her his picture, and this, to do him honor, she had framed in gold and crimson velvet.

On Christmas day he arrived in Havana. There his mother and two brothers came, summoned by the news that he had not rallied as they had hoped he would. Less than two months later he died.

The day Kane sailed for Europe, Melville, depleted by the writing of *Moby-Dick* and depressed at its poor reception, also left, but on a different ship. Melville had written Hawthorne:

Until I was twenty-five, I had no development at all. From my twenty-fifth year I date my life. Three weeks have scarcely passed between then and now, that I have not unfolded within myself. But I now feel that I am come to the inmost leaf of the bulb, and that shortly the flower must come to the mold.

The words were Melville's; they might also have been said by Kane.

X I I

Kane's Legacy

ELISHA KENT KANE belongs to the American
frontier. He did not cut a Wilderness Road which settlers
coming after him would widen into a thoroughfare leading
to new populated communities; and even the whaling
fleets which would have steered north to exploit the whale-
rich waters of Kane Basin were stricken and withered
away. Almost a hundred years passed and a new era was
born before the Arctic Ocean became strategically important as the Mediterranean of the North.

Kane's geographical discoveries seemed, in the immediate aftermath, to count for little. The hold that the Arctic
exerted over men's imaginations during the days of the
Franklin search and the Grinnell expeditions was blotted
out by the battle smoke that soon enveloped the nation.
At the same time, whaling suffered a series of blows that
leveled the industry.

The need for whale oil almost disappeared after 1859
when petroleum was found in Pennsylvania; and the

whaling fleet itself was a major casualty of the Civil War, sunk by Confederate cruisers or turned to the use of the Federal navy. With the ruin and virtual extinction of whaling, Kane Basin lost its economic significance. Less and less did fleets sail through Davis Strait and brave the terror of Melville Bay.

Only a handful of men interested in discovery extended Kane's work. The most persistent and most famous was Robert E. Peary, U.S.N. In several ways he was Kane's heir: he traced the northern coastline of Greenland and so proved its insularity; he carried Arctic logistics and sledging to their ultimate perfection, to reach the North Pole; his navigator, Captain "Bob" Bartlett, maneuvered the steamer *Roosevelt* to a harbor on Ellesmere Island, facing the polar sea; and he happily continued the living-working relations Kane had started with the Etah Eskimos.

As Kane's geographical discoveries were utilized by only a few men until aviation again made them nationally valuable, so his other scientific contribution was disregarded until biochemistry isolated those enzymes called vitamins and explained scurvy as a lack of Vitamin C. Kane's work on diet was neglected because of the tyranny of habitual atttitudes and thinking. *Arctic Explorations* gave brilliant, cogent arguments for accepting the Eskimo way of life while in the Arctic. Repeatedly Kane discussed the expedition's diet and stressed the extraordinary benefits fresh meat and raw meat had conferred on the men's well-being.

Adopting the Eskimos' eating habits was analagous to

the land explorers' reliance on their Indian guides' sure knowledge of their country. As an American, Kane knew that the pioneers lived and starved as did the Indians around them — but they did not sicken and die of scurvy. But his method offended the code adhered to by the British Admiralty, the leader in Arctic exploration, as Semmelweis offended when he insisted that mothers would not die of puerperal infection if doctors would only scrub their hands. How could British naval leaders pay attention to a man — himself a naval officer — who had disavowed naval discipline; how could they understand motivations that stemmed from the frontier where no man was master and where if a group had a leader it was a recognition of innate qualities, not because of a superimposed authority? The admirals and captains applauded Kane's heroism, but dismissed him as eccentric when he advocated junking the kinds of provisions with which Arctic-bound ships were provided and eating the health-giving animals which the Arctic offered so bountifully to the hunter. The Admiralty replaced sails with steam — but the steamers were stocked with canned meat and salt meat. As late as 1875, scurvy almost brought tragedy to the Nares Expedition that explored north of Kane Basin.

What then were the immediate results of Kane's work? Did anything survive the quick succession of blows — Kane's death, the collapse of the whaling industry, the outbreak of civil war, the intransigence of the official British attitude? Only an idea, intangible, indestructible, remained: Kane gave the world an Arctic robbed of its terrors and dangers. He had wintered at a higher latitude than any American or European and he had mastered an environment that was exclusively Arctic.

It was his original point of view that framed his charming precise disquisitions on Arctic meats. In these passages he introduced Americans to the satisfying sealiness of seal stew, the staying power of walrus steaks, the energy- and heat-giving virtues of blubber gulped raw. He attempted to overcome the usual repugnance to strange, bizarre foods and to shake the reader from a rigid allegiance to traditional eating habits. He invited Americans to face the Arctic without fear and prepared them to accept its teeming marine animals as proper nourishment. Similarly, he sought to lift the dread from the Arctic's long winter night which bleached men's spirits as it did their faces. He presented it as the season when the ice was most excellent for travel, when Eskimo families visited from settlement to settlement, sledging quickly the entire length of their coastal strip. (For his readers who lived north of the frost line, and had always preferred the surface winter laid down over their mud-bound roads, this made an easy equation between their own world and that of the distant Arctic.)

Perhaps the children whom Kane included in his audience grew up having learned that only their attitude prevented Americans from settling a region whose physical idiom was unfamiliar. "The Great American Desert," the name given to the vast interior plains that stretched from the Mississippi westward to the mountains, the plains the pioneers crossed but did not settle, was the last of the continental frontiers in time. The Great American Desert — it was so libeled on maps — expressed the backwoodsman's reaction to a region where his ax, the symbol of the cleared settlement, was useless. Did Kane, when he humanized the northernmost frontier, persuade people that the plains needed but new techniques for its bounty to express itself? Kane's idea was both indestructible and contagious.

Applying Melville's words to himself, Kane might have dated his life from his thirtieth year — only in his last seven years did he find fulfillment. Kane's work fell in that marvelous decade which, following the conquest of California, saw the "whole out-flowering of the American tradition." Compressed into that short span are the greater works of Hawthorne, Melville and Whitman, men of genius, preoccupied "with strange or rebellious types who left tradition behind."

Kane was not a writer, though his writing has vigor, distinction, and intensity; but, as an explorer, he was concerned with identical facts and values. He was kin to the writers in his "indwelling and self-aware" quality. His dramatic questing was an unconscious expression of inner search. A great explorer of the inner man, Thoreau, in an act starkly reasoned and deliberate, turned his back on civilization and rejected the conventions of his society. His words, like his gestures, had the uncompromising moral and intellectual stature of the prophet.

Neither genius nor prophet, Kane found another way

to escape from his society; only by comparison could he question its values. His ceaseless, far-flung travels were a kind of flight, as his endorsement of the Eskimo way of life was an inarticulate denial of his own world. That world used a compass oriented to influence and power, wealth and position. Kane eschewed politics and a naval career; he ran out on a successful practice; he attached himself to intangibles which promised neither distinction nor riches — the search for Franklin, the search for the open polar sea — and, ironically, achieved both.

Kane's explorations have meanings far below the surface. The conclusion of *Walden* (1854) illuminates those shadowed spaces. (How topical are its figures of speech!)

> Direct your eye right inward, and you'll find
> A thousand regions in your mind
> Yet undiscovered. Travel them, and be
> Expert in home-cosmography.

Is it the source of the Nile, or the Niger, or the Mississippi, or a Northwest Passage around this continent, that we would find? Are these the problems which most concern mankind? Is Franklin the only man who is lost, that his wife should be so earnest to find him? Does Mr. Grinnell know where he himself is? . . . Be a Columbus to whole new continents and worlds within you, opening new channels, not of trade, but of thought. Every man is the lord of a realm beside which the earthly empire of the Czar is but a petty state, a hummock left by the ice. Yet some can be patriotic who have no self-respect, and sacrifice the greater to the less. They love the soil which makes their graves, but have no sympathy with the spirit which may still animate their clay. Patriotism is a maggot in their heads. What was the meaning of that South-Sea Exploring Expedition, with all its parade and expense, but an indirect recognition of the fact that there are continents and seas in the moral world to which every man is an isthmus or an inlet, yet unexplored by him, but that it is easier to sail many thousand miles through cold and storm and cannibals, in a government ship, with five hundred men and boys to assist one, than it is to explore the private sea, the Atlantic and Pacific Ocean of one's being alone.

The unknown eulogist speaking to the listening crowd over the coffin in which lay the still-young explorer discerned the quixotic nature of Kane's life: "He lived without influence, and died without power." But one word must be added: for Kane, there was no other way he could stay home. He was fortunate in dying in the high noon of his glory.

A Note on the Sources

P ARADOXICALLY, books on exploration belong more
to the world of ideas than to that of action. The explorer's
primary concern is with the theory which motivated his search;
to this he relates his reaction to new sights and conditions; his
adventures merely embroider the ideas which preoccupy him.
Kane's books illustrate this most aptly. His sharp eye and
equally sharp pen are concentrated on strange sights and fast-
moving, exciting events, but scenes and events are always
securely tethered to intellectual concepts. His trained mind
was constantly alerted for inquiry. His books bear the stamp
of his rich personality; in them he reveals himself fully: Elisha
Kent Kane, *The United States Grinnell Expedition in Search
of Sir John Franklin* (1853) and *Arctic Explorations: The
Second Grinnell Expedition in Search of Sir John Franklin . . .
1853, '54, '55* (1856).

Of the books written about Kane, there is a sketch by his
pastor and brother-in-law, Professor Charles W. Shields, included in Kane's second book. William Elder's *Biography of
Elisha Kent Kane* (1858) is useful. Elder had the assistance of
Kane's family and friends, but his ornate style and elaboration
of details of contemporary significance are hurdles for the
modern reader. William C. Godfrey's *Narrative of the Last
Grinnell Arctic Exploring Expedition* (1857) and August Sonn-

tag's *Professor Sonntag's Narrative of the Grinnell Exploring Expedition* (1857) (queried in the catalogue as an imposture) are some of the books rushed into print at the time of Kane's death. Lastly, there is the curious volume *The Love Life of Dr. Kane . . . and Margaret Fox* (1866) which attempts to prove that Kane contracted a common-law marriage with the famous toe-tapping spiritualist from Rochester. The claim to romantic attachment to the long-dead Kane seems to have been part of Margaret Fox's frantic efforts to keep the public spotlight on her waning popularity. Kane's work as part of the grand design of Arctic exploration is dealt with in Jeannette Mirsky, *To The Arctic!* (1948).

Kane influenced subsequent explorers. See especially Charles Francis Hall, *Arctic Researches and Life among the Esquimaux* (1865) and V. Stefansson, *My Life with the Eskimo* (1913) and *The Friendly Arctic* (1921).

Literature on the seafaring frontier is voluminous but it must be pieced together out of its separate parts — the coastal trade and merchant marine, the fishing and whaling industries, the growth of shipyards and the building of clipper ships, the works of Bowditch and Maury, and regional studies and accounts of New Bedford, Nantucket, and Stonington. A few of the most accessible books follow; for the rest, the interested reader can readily set his own course: S. E. Morison, *The Maritime History of Massachusetts* (1921); G. C. Homans-S. E. Morison, *Massachusetts on the Sea 1630–1930* (1930); E. P. Hohman, *The American Whaleman* (1928); A. Laing, *Clipper Ship Men* (1944); E. S. Balch, *Antarctica* (1902); R. H. Brown, *Mirror for Americans: Likeness of the Eastern Seaboard 1810* (1943); W. O. Stevens, *Nantucket: The Far-away Island* (1936).

Scattered throughout the wealth of information and advice offered to sailing-ship captains are wonderful vignettes of particular ships in M. F. Maury's *Explanations and Sailing Directions . . . to Wind and Weather Charts* (7th ed., 1856). R. H. Dana *Two Years before the Mast* (1840). Dana's voyage begun in 1834 is a fine account of one man's experience in the merchant marine during the 1830's when the New York to San Francisco run by way of the Straits of Magellan was part of American thrust and enterprise. And last — or first — is the only literary masterpiece written by someone who was part of this frontier: Herman Melville's *Moby-Dick or the White Whale.*

INDEX

Index